PRESSURE CANNING

&

WATER BATH CANNING

FOR THE MODERN

HOMESTEADER

(2 Books in 1):

Comprehensive Beginner Guides to Food Preservation, Storage, and Delicious Recipes
- Featuring Over 100 Starter Recipes

Elizabeth Ash

Table of contents

Book 1: *PRESSURE CANNING FOR THE MODERN HOMESTEADER* -------- *1*

Introduction -- *3*

Chapter 1: -- *6*

  Pressure Canning Basics -- **6**

    How Does Pressure Canning Work? --- 6

    How Does Pressure Canning Differ From Other Food Preservation Methods? -------------------- 7

    Benefits of Pressure Canning --- 8

    Possible Risks of Pressure Canning -- 10

Chapter 2: --- *12*

  Best and Worst Foods to Preserve Through Pressure Canning ------------------------- **12**

    The Best Foods to Preserve -- 12

    The Worst Foods to Preserve (and Why) --- 15

Chapter 3: --- *18*

  How to Start --- **18**

    Basic Equipment Needed -- 18

    Getting Started With Pressure Canning --- 19

Chapter 4: --- *24*

  Focusing on Safety --- **24**

    Common Pressure Canning Mistakes to Avoid --------------------------------------- 24

    Essential Safety Tips to Keep In Mind -- 26

Chapter 5: --- *28*

  Building Your Prepper Pantry With Pressure-Canned Goods ------------------------- **28**

    The Benefits of Having a Prepper's Pantry --- 28

    Tips for Planning Your Prepper Pantry --- 29

  All About Meal Planning and How to Start -- **33**

Chapter 6: --- *36*

  Recipes for Pressure Canning Meats -- **36**

    Why Pressure Canning for Meats is Important ------------------------------------- 36

    Safety First: Considerations for Meat Canning ------------------------------------- 36

    5 Essential Tips for Pressure Canning Meats -------------------------------------- 36

Pressure Canning Beef: A Comprehensive Guide----------------------------------37

Recommended Processing Times and Pressures for Chunks of Beef----------------------------38

Beef Pot Roast--- 40

Beef Short Rib--- 41

Pressure Canning Pork: Your Complete Guide ----------------------------- 44

Pressure-Canned Pork --- 46

Pulled Pork --- 48

Pressure Canning Chicken: Your Comprehensive Guide ----------------------- 50

Canned Chicken and Gravy-- 53

Canned Chicken Recipe--- 56

Pressure Canning Fish and Tuna ----------------------------------- 59

Tuna-- 60

Chapter 7: -- 62

Recipes for Pressure Canning Vegetables--------------------------- 62

Carrots--- 63

Corn Cream-Style Recipe--- 66

Whole Corn Kernels Recipe--------------------------------------- 68

Peas-- 70

Sweet Potatoes --- 73

Pressure Canning White Potatoes --------------------------------- 76

Spinach -- 79

Pressure Canning Baked Beans ------------------------------------ 82

Beans with Tomato or Molasses Sauce----------------------------- 85

Pressure Canning Fresh Lima Beans ------------------------------- 87

Pressure Canning Snap and Italian Beans -------------------------- 90

Okra--- 93

Pumpkins or Winter Squash -------------------------------------- 96

Mixed Vegetables--- 99

Chapter 8: -- *102*

   Recipes for Pressure Canning Soups and Stews ----------------102

   Chicken Soup--102

   Pressure-Canned Chicken Stock ---------------------------106

   Beef Stew ---109

   Beef Stock --112

   Vegetable Soup--115

   Pressure-Canned Lentil Soup------------------------------118

   Chili --121

   Basic Chili for Variety-----------------------------------124

Chapter 9: -- *127*

   Recipes for Pressure Canning Seafood---------------------127

   Clams --127

   Shrimp--130

   Oyster --134

   Crabs---138

   Smoked Fish ---142

   Salmon ---145

Chapter 10-- *148*

   Other Pressure Canning Recipes to Try--------------------148

   Salsa ---148

   Spaghetti Sauce ---152

   Tomato Juice --155

Conclusion --- *158*

   Mastering the Art of Pressure Canning -------------------158

References--- *160*

Book 2: *Water Bath Canning & Preserving for Beginners* ------------------------ *164*

A Step-By-Step Guide To Start Your Own Preservative-Free Prepper Pantry - Featuring 55 Starter Recipes To Can Fruits, Vegetables, Jams, Sauces, And More -------------------------- 164

© Copyright 2022 - All rights reserved. -- 165

Legal Notice: --- 165

Disclaimer Notice: --- 165

Introduction --- *166*

The Wonders of Water Bath Canning --- 166

Chapter 1 --- *169*

Water Bath Canning Basics --**169**

How Does Water Bath Canning Work? -- 169

How Does Water Bath Canning Differ From Other Food Preservation Methods -------------- 170

Water Bath Canning -- 171

Atmospheric Steam Canning -- 171

Pressure Canning -- 172

BENEFITS OF WATER BATH CANNING -- 173

It's a Very Simple and Safe Procedure -- 173

Eliminates Bacteria That Causes Food Spoilage ------------------------------------ 173

Allows You to Preserve Certain Low-Acid Foods Through Proper Processing -------------- 174

Creates a Vacuum Inside the Jars to Keep the Contents Preserved ---------------------- 174

Ensures a Long Shelf-Life -- 174

POSSIBLE RISKS OF WATER BATH CANNING ---------------------------------- 175

Contamination Through Unsterilized Tools ------------------------------------ 175

Reusing Old Lids -- 175

The Danger of Improperly Canning Low-Acid Foods ------------------------------ 176

Botulism --- 176

Chapter 2 --- *178*

Best and Worst Foods to Preserve Through Water Bath Canning --------------------**178**

THE BEST FOODS TO PRESERVE -- 178

Fruits --- 179

Jams and Jellies -- 179

Pickled or Fermented Foods -- 179

Relishes, Chutneys, Pie Fillings, Juices, and More -------------------------------- 180

Salsas and Sauces -- 180

Tomatoes --- 180

Vegetables --- 181

THE WORST FOODS TO PRESERVE (AND WHY) -------------------------------- 181

Meat, Poultry, and Seafood -- 182

Most Types of Veggies -- 182

Soup --- 182

Vegetable, Meat, Poultry, or Seafood Stock ------------------------------------ 183

Dairy Products--- 183

Chapter 3 -- *184*

How to Start --**184**
BASIC EQUIPMENT NEEDED --- 184
Pot--- 184
Canning Jars -- 185
Canning Lids -- 185
Rings-- 185
Canning Rack-- 186
Other Tools and Equipment --- 186
GETTING STARTED WITH WATER BATH CANNING ------------------------------ 187
Plan Before You Process-- 187
Read the Recipe Carefully Before You Start--- 187
Sterilize the Jars, but Not the Lids -- 188
Fill the Pot With Enough Water--- 188
Know the Basic Water Bath Canning Steps --- 188
Make Sure There is Enough Headspace -- 189
Take Note of Processing Times and Altitudes --- 190
Take Note of the Differences Between Raw and Hot Pack Preservation ------------ 190
Use New Lids Each Time You Process and Remove the Rings Before Storage--------------- 191
Make Sure That the Jars are Sealed Properly-- 191
Label and Store the Jars Properly --- 191
Wash All of Your Tools and Equipment After Use ------------------------------------ 192
Never Make Up Your Own Canning Recipes --- 192

Chapter 4 -- *193*

Preparing Your Prepper Pantry --**193**
THE BENEFITS OF HAVING A PREPPER PANTRY ------------------------------- 193
Food Security-- 194
Peace of Mind -- 194
Convenience -- 194
Customization -- 195
TIPS FOR PLANNING YOUR PREPPER PANTRY------------------------------- 195
Create a Plan--- 195
Determine the Location of Your Prepper Pantry------------------------------------- 196
Build Your Prepper Pantry Gradually --- 196
Come Up With a Budget--- 196
Focus on Nutrition and Variety --- 197
Rotate Your Stocks -- 197
Start Meal Planning--- 198
ALL ABOUT MEAL PLANNING AND HOW TO START------------------------- 198

Chapter 5 --- *201*

Recipes for Canning Fruits---201

APRICOTS --201

Blackberries ---203

Cherries ---205

Cranberries ---207

Fruit Cocktail ---209

Grapes ---211

Kiwi ---213

Lemons --215

Mango---217

Peaches --219

Pears ---221

Plums---223

Raspberries --225

Chapter 6 --- *227*

Recipes for Canning Vegetables---227

Candied Jalapeños --227

Dill Pickles --229

Mushrooms --231

Pickled Asparagus---233

Pickled Beets ---235

Pickled Carrots --237

Pickled Eggplants ---239

Pickled Green Beans--241

Pickled Mixed Veggies---243

Pickled Onions ---245

Spicy Pickled Garlic --247

Tomatoes --249

Chapter 7 --- *251*

Recipes for Canning Jams and Jellies------------------251

3-Berry Jam --251

Coconut and Pineapple Jam----------------------------253

Orange and Fig Jam ------------------------------------255

Salted Cantaloupe Jam---------------------------------257

Zucchini Jam ---259

Corn Cob Jelly ---261

Dandelion Jelly --263

Mint Jelly---265

Spicy Pepper Jelly -------------------------------------268

Watermelon Jelly --------------------------------------270

Chapter 8 --- *272*

Recipes for Canning Salsas and Sauces----------------272

Apple and Peach Salsa---------------------------------272

Classic Tomato Salsa ----------------------------------275

Roasted Spicy Salsa ------------------------------------278

Salsa Verde ---281

Sweet Strawberry Salsa --------------------------------284

Barbeque Sauce--286

Chocolate and Raspberry Sauce ----------------------289

Pear Sauce with Vanilla and Caramel ----------------291

Pizza Sauce---293

Spicy Pepper Sauce ------------------------------------295

Chapter 9 --- *298*

Other Canning Recipes to Try-------------------------298

Ketchup---298

Wholegrain Mustard --301

Pickle Relish ---303

Sweet Corn Relish ---305

Apple Pie Filling --308

Sweet Pecan Pie Filling --311

Date and Banana Chutney --313

Green Tomato Chutney --315

Vegetable Juice --317

Sauerkraut ---319

Chapter 10 --- *321*

Focusing on Safety --321

COMMON WATER BATH CANNING MISTAKES TO AVOID ------------------------------ 321

Not Starting With High-Quality Ingredients --- 321

Using a Water Bath Canner for Foods That Need to Be Pressure Canned --------------------- 322

Using the Wrong Size of Canning Jars --- 322

Using Damaged Canning Jars --- 322

Removing Air Bubbles With a Metal Spoon--- 322

Not Adding Enough Water to the Pot--- 323

Not Considering Your Altitude --- 323

Taking the Jars Out of the Canner Right After Processing--------------------------------- 323

Storing the Jars Without Removing the Rings--- 323

Not Labeling Your Jars --- 324

Essential Safety Tips to Keep in Mind ---325

Conclusion -- *326*

Water Bath Canning Like a Pro ---326

References -- *328*

Image References --- *337*

PRESSURE CANNING FOR THE MODERN HOMESTEADER

A Comprehensive Beginner's Guide To Food Preservation, Storage, And Delicious Recipes

Introduction

We need food to sustain our lives. Without food, our body will fail to function as it normally does, which will result in sickness and, worse, death. With this, we can all agree that food is a significant aspect of our lives. If we want to live life to the fullest, we need to ensure that our body is getting enough nutrients to sustain its biological functions. This means that it is our responsibility to supply ourselves with healthy and sustainable food. This responsibility is not only dependent on the food and agriculture industries. You, on your own, can produce quality, healthy, and sustainable food in your home.

Without proper handling and management, food can go bad. This is a situation called food waste that you shouldn't allow to happen. Food waste is when food intended for human consumption is lost or wasted (Lai, 2021). This can happen at any stage of the supply chain, from harvest to transport, market, and home consumption. For instance, if you live in an area with frequent power outages, freezer meals may not be a good idea for your meal plans. Thus, you should learn how to store and preserve your food, as food wasted is money wasted.

Food waste is a serious problem, as about one-third of global food supplies are wasted. This accounts for approximately 2.5 billion metric tons of food waste worldwide every year (Lai, 2021). You may be unable to imagine how much food that is. How can we waste so much food despite 811 million people suffering from hunger worldwide in 2020 (United Nations, n.d.)? With food waste and food shortages, everyone must be equipped with the necessary skills to store and preserve food. In fact, with the huge amount of food waste every year, the problem may not be about food shortages but rather food storage, handling, and management, among others. It is high time to make a change. Start by learning how to properly store and preserve your own food so you can reduce your annual food waste. By doing so, you are not only helping yourself, but you are also helping create a change in the environment, global and national economies, food security, and nutrition.

In terms of nutrition, by preserving your own food, you can be sure that the food you produce is a healthier option than commercially-produced preserved foods. By preserving food yourself, you can control the quantity and quality of ingredients in your recipe. This means that you can adjust the recipe based on your dietary needs and how you want to enjoy your food. In addition, you will be safe from any harmful amounts of natural and artificial preservatives present in commercially preserved foods. For instance, if the preserved food you consume includes too many natural preservatives like sugar or salt, it can pose harm to your health. Some preserved foods, like one serving of commercial beef jerky, contain about 470 mg of sodium, which is already 20% of the daily recommended intake. Meanwhile, there are also artificial preservatives used in commercially preserved food, which are chemicals like potassium sorbate and parabens. Artificial preservatives are often used in processed foods that should only be eaten in moderation (Hoory, 2021). With the danger of too much consumption of food preservatives, you should consider preserving your own food to make it more healthy and made of higher-quality ingredients.

An excellent way to preserve your own food is by pressure canning it. Learning pressure canning is life-changing. Aside from gaining knowledge on food production and food processing, you will also learn how to care for yourself better. You will know which foods and food combinations will provide your body with the quality nutrients it needs to function. Knowing how to take care of your body is an important life skill you should learn. You can start by learning how to cook and exploring recipes that are good for your body. Upon learning pressure canning, I have understood how my body functions and what nutrients it needs to remain healthy. I have also learned which ingredients enhance the flavor of each recipe and which ingredients to combine to create certain flavors. In general, I can say that I am living a healthier and happier life with the help of pressure canning. Now, I am enjoying most of my meals because of the food production and food processing skills I learned along the way.

Pressure canning involves the use of a pressure cooker that heats water to produce very hot steam, making the temperature inside the cooker as hot as 266° F (130° C). This high temperature, much higher than the maximum heat possible in other cooking equipment, can penetrate food quickly without reducing the vitamin and mineral content (The Canning Diva, n.d.).

With this book, you will learn the science behind pressure canning and the safety precautions you must be aware of. To be specific, you will learn about the benefits of pressure canning as well as the possible risks associated with it, so you will know how to safely employ this preservation method. Then, you will be provided with a list and explanation of which foods are best and worst when it comes to preserving through pressure canning. Upon learning the general idea, you need the basics. Hence, you will learn the equipment you need for pressure canning as well as the steps you need to follow so you can safely and effectively preserve your food for future consumption. In addition, you should also be made aware of common pressure canning mistakes you should avoid making, including safety tips you should learn by heart.

After you have learned the foundation and the basics, you will find guidelines on how to build your own prepper pantry with pressure-canned goods in this book, which includes the planning and organizing skills you need for the efficient storage of your pressure-canned goods. Of course, it should not end there; you should also learn some recipes you can adopt and explore, such as recipes for pressure canning meats, vegetables, soups and stews, seafood, and other interesting recipes to try.

Pressure canning is a versatile and beneficial food preservation method. It can help you take care of yourself and your family, as well as the environment. Pressure canning is easy and cost-effective, saving you money from food waste. Learning pressure canning skills is a good investment for your future. Get ready to learn how to pressure can and explore recipes that will sustain your health and that you will enjoy eating.

Chapter 1:

PRESSURE CANNING BASICS

Preserving your own food is not a hard task. It is a skill that can be easily learned and refined with practice. It doesn't need to be complicated; just focus on the goal of preserving and storing your own food, which will further lead to improved health. I know that the process of canning your own food can be overwhelming, but rest assured that you will be provided with the necessary lessons, tips, and strategies that you will need. After all, pressure canning is a safe and cost-effective method of preserving food. This is especially practiced by home gardeners and other enthusiastic food people aiming for food sustainability and efficiency. If you are one of them, here are the basics that you need to know:

How Does Pressure Canning Work?

Opting to preserve your own food allows you to control the quality of the food you serve to your family. You can surely ensure that the food on your table is healthy for your family as long as you follow the guidelines for operating a pressure canner and use high-quality supplies, equipment, and ingredients. The use of pressure canning methods ensures that harmful bacteria are killed, especially in low-acid foods like meats, poultry, and dairy. A pressure canner has the capacity to reach and maintain 240° F through steam under pressure, which can kill bad bacteria. By pressure canning, you can preserve fruits and vegetables beyond their season, as well as meat, without the need to refrigerate it.

To become familiar with pressure canning, let us discuss pressure canners first. Primarily, a pressure canner has eight parts, as follows (Utah State University, n.d.):

- Pressure Dial Gauge: This registers the pressure in either pounds or metric. It has a pointer that indicates the pressure inside the canner. If the pressure differs from what is expected, you can adjust it through the heat setting.

- Pressure regulator: This part is a safety device that prevents the pressure from building or reaching more than 15 lbs inside the canner.

- Canning rack: This is located on the bottom of the canner and functions as a holder for jars. This part must always be used when canning.

- Vent pipe: This serves as a pathway where steam can escape from the inside of the canner while exhausting—ensuring that all air escapes from the canner as the presence of air affects the temperature inside the canner, further leading to an inaccurate pressure reading (Pazzaglia, 2018).

- Air vent: This is also called the cover lock and automatically exhausts air from the canner. It also works as a visual indication of the pressure inside the canner.

- Sealing ring: This is a gasket placed into the canner cover and works by securing a pressure-tight seal between the cover and the body of the canner during canning. However, some types or brands of pressure canners do not have this feature, such as those with screw-down covers.

- Overpressure plug: This part is seen in the canner cover. It works by automatically popping out or releasing steam when the vent pipe is clogged. Thus, it functions as an exhaust or vent when the vent pipe becomes dysfunctional.

- Locking bracket: As the name suggests, it locks the canner. It is located inside the canner, where the canner body engages with the air vent. It locks the canner, so it prevents the cover from being opened when there is pressure inside. Some types of pressure canners do not have this feature.

How Does Pressure Canning Differ From Other Food Preservation Methods?

Canning works by removing air and killing enzymes so the growth of bad bacteria, yeasts, and molds can be prevented. There are two types of canning methods: one is water bathing, and the other uses pressure. The pH-level, or acidity, of the food to be preserved dictates which method should be used. First, you should know the difference between acidic and low-acid foods.

Acidic foods or those with a low pH contain enough acid to prevent bacterial growth. This type of food includes fruits, sauerkraut, pickles, marmalades, jellies, jams, and fruit batter. These foods and recipes can be preserved through bath canning, which doesn't require pressure. Meanwhile, low-acid foods have a high pH. They do not contain enough acid to prevent the growth of bacteria. These low-acid foods can be the perfect host for a deadly bacteria called Botulinum, which is odorless, invisible, and tasteless. Botulinum can cause botulism, which is a rare and deadly disease that causes symptoms such as blurry vision, double vision, difficulty swallowing, muscle weakness, drooping eyelids, slurred speech, difficulty moving the eyes, and difficulty breathing (Centers for Disease Control and Prevention, 2021). Low-acid foods include milk, grains, meat, seafood, and almost all vegetables. For both water bath and pressure canning, the exact temperature, processing time, or pressure depends on the kind of food, the recipe, and the size of the jar being canned.

Aside from canning, there are also other methods to preserve food, including curing, drying, smoking, freezing, pickling, and fermenting (Desrosier *et al.*, 2023). Curing involves the use of sugar, vinegar, sodium nitrate, or sodium chloride to stop the growth of spoilage bacteria. However, there are only a limited number of foods that can be cured or pickled. Drying and smoking are methods of dehydration. The loss of moisture content in dehydrated foods increases the concentration of nutrients in the food mass. Yet, in some cases, toxin-producing bacteria were still able to withstand the low-moisture environment, which may cause food poisoning when the dehydrated products are rehydrated and eaten. Meanwhile, freezing involves putting fresh produce at a temperature that is below 0° C (32° F). However, freezing may result in lost quality, and frozen products may experience a loss in hydration when thawed. Fermenting and pickling are chemical processes where molecules like glucose are broken down through anaerobic methods with the use of a watery solution that is sometimes mixed with salt. Only plant-based produce can be fermented or pickled.

With the provided description of other preserving methods, it can be concluded that there are a lot of foods and recipes that you can preserve using this pressure canning method. In addition, you can adjust the recipe of your preserved foods according to your dietary needs and taste.

Benefits of Pressure Canning

The main benefit of utilizing pressure canning is that it will allow you to preserve foods, even those that are low-acid. You may even preserve stews, chili, and spaghetti sauces, among others, through pressure canning. Yet there are also other benefits you can reap from pressure canning your food at home, such as the following:

- Variety: It can safely preserve foods that a water bath can't, such as low-acid foods. You can even combine low-acid foods with acidic ones.

- Creativity: Pressure canning will allow you to preserve foods that you never thought you could preserve. This preservation method will enable you to be creative with the food and recipes you preserve, given that you have followed safety precautions and are careful with your recipe.

- Flexibility: Not all people need and follow the same diet. There are people who need a special diet, such as a low-sodium diet. With pressure canning, you can preserve food according to a recipe that fits your dietary needs. In addition, you may also preserve foods that you like eating. For instance, if you love eating pasta, you can pressure cook some pasta sauces that you like.

- Time-efficient: Although the process of pressure canning takes time, it is still efficient and time-saving. You can dedicate a day every month or so to preserving some of your favorite foods and meals that you can consume even after one to five years. For example, you can spend a few hours pressure canning a dozen servings of pasta sauce that you can easily serve to your family when you don't have time to cook in the future. In addition, pressure canning requires less processing time than a water bath. For instance, tomatoes should be processed for 45 minutes when following the water bath method, but it will only take 10 minutes to process them in a pressure canner.

- Tenderizes meat: Pressure canning does not only preserve meat; it can also tenderize it. In addition, pressure-canned meat can be used in many recipes, like nacho dip, rice dishes, and pasta sauces.

- Electricity-efficient: Pressure-canned goods do not need refrigeration to last longer. You can just store your pressure-canned goods in your pantry. This means that even if you lose electricity for a period of time, you have the assurance that your food stock will not go bad.

- Better quality compared to commercial canned goods: If you process your own foods, you can ensure that they do not contain any additives like MSG that can be unhealthy for you and your family. You can also make sure that the ingredients used in your food are of high quality.

Possible Risks of Pressure Canning

Home canning is an efficient way to preserve food that you can share with your family and friends. However, if not done correctly, it can pose risks that are sometimes deadly. The food-borne disease called botulism should be the number one concern in terms of safety. The goal of your home canning must be the prevention of the growth of Botulinum and other harmful bacteria. If you do not follow safety precautions, your canned goods may put you at risk of botulism. The environment that allows the growth of Botulinum is one that is moist and low in acid, with a temperature of between 40° and 120° F and less than 2% oxygen. The spores of Botulinum can hardly be destroyed at boiling temperature, so a pressure canner with a higher temperature has the capability to destroy them as long as you follow safety precautions and safe recipes. Such precautions include not adding starches, which slow the penetration of heat, and adding too many vegetables to salsas and sauces, which further drops the acidity.

Elevation, or altitude, also plays an important role in pressure canning. Altitude refers to the height of an object relative to ground level. This is important because the higher you are above sea level, the less air is pressing you down, which is measured through air pressure. Another thing you should understand is that air pressure affects the boiling temperature of the water. The higher the altitude, the lower the air pressure, which allows water to boil at a lower temperature. Hence, it is important to adjust your temperature when pressure canning according to the altitude of your area so that you achieve the right and safe environment for food preservation.

Another cause of concern when home canning is the use of contaminated tools and equipment. When it comes to tools such as canning jars, it is not enough to just wash and dry them. Home canning can only be safe if you sterilize your cans to minimize the risk of toxin growth. Aside from your canning jars, you should also sterilize your tongs and other canning tools to avoid cross-contamination. More importantly, you will put yourself and your family at great risk if you reuse your lids. Pressure canning lids must include a rubber ring around them for the can to seal properly; this rubber ring is only suitable for one canning use.

Some common signs that your canned goods are no longer safe to consume include the following:

- The outside of the jar has leaks, cracks, or swollen spots.

- When you open the canned jar, you don't hear a pop or suction noise.

- You see signs of bacterial growth on the underside of the jar.

- There is an odd liquid or foam at the top of the food.

- The food is stinky, discolored, or moldy.

Pressure canning is an efficient and safe way to preserve food. Knowing the basics and foundation of pressure canning is important before you can get started. The next piece of knowledge you should gain about pressure canning is what kinds of foods you can and cannot preserve through pressure canning.

Chapter 2:

BEST AND WORST FOODS TO PRESERVE THROUGH PRESSURE CANNING

I've always love how food preserves a memory. –Piolo Pascual

The beauty of pressure canning is that you can preserve a lot of food and various recipes, even those with low acidity. Yet, it is important to remember that there are foods that are best preserved using pressure canning, and there are some that are not suitable for this method. When making your own food, always prioritize your safety. Thus, it is best to know which foods can and cannot be preserved through pressure canning. In addition, learning which foods can be pressure-canned will help you understand this preservation technique as well as the science behind it.

The Best Foods to Preserve

The level of acidity in food will dictate how it should be processed for preservation. Acidity is measured by pH. The lower the pH, the more acidic the food. Foods with a pH of 4.6 or higher are considered low-acid foods. The types of foods that can be safely preserved through pressure canning are vegetables, stews, stocks, soups, broths, meat, poultry, chili, fish, and baked beans. Here are more in-depth discussions of pressure canning these food types:

- **Vegetables**: Vegetables go bad fast. If you are a gardener or have a lot of vegetable supplies, it will be more efficient for you if you preserve your vegetables through pressure canning. Preserving your vegetables can help during unpredictable food shortages, the rising cost of agricultural products, and supply chain issues. To be specific, here is a list of vegetables that can be pressure-canned:

  ○ asparagus

- spinach

- beans or peas

- Swiss chard

- onion

- peppers

- carrots

- corn

- parsnip

- turnip greens

- kale

- mixed vegetables

- mushroom

- pumpkins

- okra

- potatoes

- succotash

- tomatillo

- Winter squash

- **Stews and soups:** Pressure canning stews and soups can be time-saving, as you just need to reheat them, and you can instantaneously serve your family dinner during hectic days. You can be flexible with the kind of stew or soup you would like canned. Here are some ideas on what stews and soups you can preserve:

  - taco soup

  - meat and vegetable soup

- mixed vegetable soup

- various stews

- **Broths and stocks:** Broths and stocks are versatile ingredients or parts of meals. We can all agree that we often use broths and stocks in various home-cooked meals. Thus, having your own preserved supply of broths and stocks will make your cooking chores easier. If you need some ideas on which broths and stocks to preserve, here are some:

  - bone broth

  - chicken stock

  - beef stock

  - pork stock

  - fish stock

  - vegetable broth

  - shrimp stock

  - organ meat stock

  - pheasant stock

- **Meat (pork, beef, poultry):** Pressure canning your meat products is a great way to diversify your food storage. It can also help you prepare your meals for the week or month. With pressure canning, you can now buy bulk meat instead of just purchasing what can fit in your freezer. This preservation method is also very helpful for people who raise their own animals. Meat products that can be pressure-canned include the following:

  - chicken

  - turkey

  - pork

  - beef

- rabbit

- venison

- **Fish and other seafood:** This food type is a healthy source of protein. You can also use the pressure canning method to preserve seafood. However, pressure canning fish and other seafood is more complicated compared to other meat products. Hence, you should follow recipes closely. Some seafood that can be pressure-canned are the following:

  - tuna

  - trout

  - clams

  - salmon

  - crab meat

  - shrimp

  - oyster

  - other fishes

- **Chili and baked beans:** For diversified food storage, you can also preserve chili and baked beans. Pressure canning these foods will allow you to provide a hearty meal to your family in a short amount of time. Pressure canning works for baked beans and homemade chili variations.

The foods listed and mentioned are safe to be pressure-canned. Just remember to follow recipes and pay attention to the quality of your ingredients.

The Worst Foods to Preserve (and Why)

There are a lot of foods and recipes that you can preserve through pressure canning. However, there are foods that are not safe to be pressure-canned. I suggest that you do not gamble with your health and avoid pressure canning these types of foods. Here is a list with an explanation of why such foods are not safe to be canned (J&R Pierce Family Farm, n.d.).

- **Cauliflower and broccoli:** Although there will be no major ill effects, they are not recommended for pressure canning. Doing so will result in the rendering of cauliflower and broccoli, making them mushy and soft. This means that pressure-canned cauliflower and broccoli are not palatable to eat. Instead, you can just pickle these vegetables.

- **Artichokes, eggplants, and olives:** Just like cauliflower and broccoli, these vegetables can become mushy when pressure-canned. In addition, pressure canning will also result in discolored and unpalatable processed artichokes, eggplants, and olives.

- **Cabbage and lettuce:** These vegetables will become too soft when pressure-canned, and you will surely not eat them. Instead, ferment or eat them fresh.

- **Squash:** Squash is too soft to be canned. Yet, it may be possible to pickle them first before water bath canning them and not pressure canning.

- **Milk:** Milk and any food products with milk, such as cheese, butter, and cream, must not be canned. Milk is too alkaline (low acid) to be pressure-canned. It is a perfect environment for the growth of botulism. In addition, the fat in milk helps preserve botulism spores when canning. Hence, pressure canning milk should never be an option.

- **Lard:** There is no reason to can lard. However, if you want to get creative with lard, do not attempt pressure canning it. Lard contains dense fat that will not allow heat penetration. Hence, pressure-canned lard can be home to harmful bacteria.

- **Cornstarch and flour:** Cornstarch, flour, and breads have the capacity to break down acidic foods. This breakdown will interfere with the killing process of harmful bacteria. Hence, they cannot be pressure-canned, or they will become host to botulism.

- **Nuts:** This food type can be a perfect host for botulism due to its oily nature. The oil in the coat of nuts will protect botulism spores against the heat.

Food should provide us with the nutrients and energy we need to function. It is not intended to harm us. Hence, you should practice preparing and processing your food safely. Do not risk yourself and your family from food poisoning, as it can be deadly. Always practice safety precautions and choose your ingredients carefully when pressure canning foods.

Now that you know which foods can and cannot be pressure-canned, get ready to get started. In the next chapter, you will be provided with relevant information you will need to know so you can get started on developing pressure canning skills that are safe for you and your family. Happy canning!

Chapter 3:

HOW TO START

A lot of us enjoy eating quality food. We all need food to survive, and we must develop a healthy relationship with it. Learning how to process and preserve your own food is a great way to improve your relationship with food. You will begin to understand which foods will improve your and your family's health and which foods you will enjoy eating. It is also a great way to save money and time. Thus, it is necessary that you start learning pressure canning. Trust me, it just sounds hard, but it is actually pretty easy. It is something that you can learn and implement quickly.

Basic Equipment Needed

Before you can safely preserve your food through pressure canning, you need to invest in some equipment and materials, such as a pressure canner and jars, among others. There is various equipment needed so you can ensure the safety of the food you will process:

- First, let's talk about jars. You can preserve food either in glass jars or metal containers. However, if you opt for metal containers, you are only allowed to use them once, and they require more specialized equipment, making them a more expensive choice. The best and most cost-effective choice you have is a regular, wide-mouth Mason-type, threaded, home-canning jar with a self-sealing lid. Usually, mason jars are available in sizes like 1/2 pint, one pint, one and a half pint, quart, and half gallon. For the jar mouth, the standard size is 2 and 3/8 inches. Yet, you can also opt for wide-mouth jars (3-inch-wide mouth) so you can fill and empty them more easily. If you carefully use and sterilize your mason jars, you can reuse them many times, provided that you use new lids for every canning process. Be careful with mayonnaise-type jars, as they are prone to jar breakage, which makes them unsafe for pressure canning.

- Learn which lid to use when pressure canning. For a more efficient process, you can use self-sealing lids. Usually, a self-sealing lid has a flat metal lid that is held in place by a metal screw band. A self-sealing lid works due to a lid gasket that softens and flows slightly so it covers the jar-sealing surface when being processed. Yet, while sealing, the gasket still allows air inside the jar to escape, so it can create a vacuum. Meanwhile, as the jar cools, the gasket will form an airtight seal. As a safety precaution, only use self-sealing jars that were manufactured within the last five years. Be careful not to use lids that are dented or deformed.

- Pressure canning requires a pressure canner. Most pressure canners are manufactured to hold about eight to nine-pint jars or seven quart jars. If you don't need to process a lot, you can invest in a small pressure canner that can usually hold four-quart jars. If you always have a big harvest or a large family to feed, you can opt for a large pressure canner that can hold 18-pint jars in two layers or seven-quart jars.

Getting Started With Pressure Canning

To get started with pressure canning, you should learn how to differentiate and implement raw-packing and hot-packing. Another important skill to consider is controlling headspace. An important factor in food safety that you should always do is jar cleaning and preparation, including sterilization and lid preparation, which will be discussed in this chapter. As a beginner, you may not know how to use a pressure canner yet. Hence, you should follow the steps for a successful pressure canning process. In addition, processing time also has a significant effect on the safety and success of your pressure canning. I will help you create guiding tables so you can easily determine the proper process time as well as temperature and pressure. I hope that you do not forget about the safety precautions of cooling jars after pressure canning them. You should also learn about testing jar seals once they have cooled down. There may be a lot to learn about pressure canning, but trust me, the learning process is worth it. Having a ready supply of your favorite food at any time makes pressure canning a worthwhile endeavor.

Before you can start pressure canning, you should identify the pre-canning processes that you should do, such as determining if you will practice hot-packing or raw-packing. Fresh foods may contain about 10 to 30% air. The amount of air removed from preserved food determines how long it can last. Raw-packing is the process where you fill your jars with fresh, unheated foods. However, if there is entrapped air in the food, it may result in discoloration within two to three months of storage. Meanwhile, hot-packing requires you to simmer your ingredients or foods for two to five minutes before filling them into your canning jars. In addition, whether the process uses raw or hot foods, the water, syrup, or sauce to be added to the jar must also be hot. This can help remove air from the food, which will keep it afloat in the jar, increasing the vacuum in the sealed jar.

Now that we are talking about filling the jars with food, you should know how much food you should put in the jar. An important concept in this process is headspace, which is the unfilled space in the canning jar. For foods to be processed in a pressure canner, it is recommended that you leave about 1 to 1 1/4 inches of headspace. The headspace is necessary for the expansion of food while it is being processed. It is also necessary for forming vacuums once the jars are cooled.

Let's shift to jar cleaning and preparation. Before you use your jars, be sure to wash them in hot water with detergent. You may either wash them by hand or in a dishwasher. You should let your jars remain hot until they are filled with food. You can do this by submerging the empty canning jars in water that is at 180° F until it is time to fill them with food. You may also sterilize your canning jars, especially if you will process pickled products. After washing and rinsing your canning jars, submerge them in water, provided that they are in a right-side-up position, in a boiling-water canner with a rack at the bottom. Ensure that the water is 1 inch above the tops of the jars. Boil it for up to 10 minutes (if your altitude is less than 1,000 feet). If you are at a higher elevation, boil it for an additional 1 minute per 1,000 feet of elevation. Then, reduce the heat and keep the jars in the water until you are ready to fill them. However, if the foods will be pressure-canned for more than 10 minutes, the jars don't need to be sterilized. In terms of lids, just remember not to retighten the lids after processing. Do not worry if it does not seem tight at first because as the jar cools down, it will form a high vacuum. This happens because the food inside will contract, which will pull the self-sealing lid firmly against the jar. Always ensure that you follow the manufacturer's guidelines so the lid will tighten properly.

Low-acid foods need pressure canning to be preserved. Usually, a pressure canner's process would last from 55 to 100 minutes. A pressure canner needs pressure to increase the temperature. A pressure canner operated at sea level needs a pressure of 10.5 lbs to create an internal temperature of 240° F. To successfully process your foods through pressure canning, here are the steps to be taken:

- Fill the canner with approximately two to three inches of hot water. Although some recipes require more water than others, be sure to check your recipe for the amount of water to be filled into the canner. Remember to put a rack inside the canner where you will place your canning jars for processing. Then, using a jar lifter, place your securely fastened canning jars filled with food on the rack in an upright position.

- Be sure to remove or leave the weight off the vent port or open the petcock while heating at the highest setting until the steam freely flows off the vent. This step is necessary to exhaust all the air from the pressure canner through the open vent. Exhaust steam for 10 minutes before placing the weight on the vent. Allow the canner to build pressure for three to five minutes.

- Once the dial gauge indicates the recommended pressure indicated in the recipe, start your timer. If you are using a weighted-gauge pressure canner, start your timer when the gauge begins to rock or jiggle. Be sure that you know the time needed to process your food beforehand. Adjust the heat so that the pressure inside the canner becomes steady in terms of pressure. Although this may be hard to achieve, you may go slightly above the correct pressure. Remember that the pressure variations must not be too big during processing, as they may result in unnecessary liquid losses in the processed jars. If there is a point when the pressure goes below the recommended pressure, increase the heat to return it back to the right pressure, then restart the timing process.

- When the timer goes off, turn off the heat to allow the canner to depressurize. Be patient with this step, as force-cooling the canner may result in spoilage. Examples of force-cooling are placing the canner under cold running water and opening the vent port. Meanwhile, if you allow a standard-size canner to cool on its own, it will take about 30 to 45 minutes. Yet, there are newer models with thinner walls that cool down faster than those with thick walls.

- Once the canner has depressurized, you can remove the weight from the vent for ten minutes before opening the canner lid. Remember to lift the lid away from your face to avoid burning your face from the steam.

- Using a jar lifter, carefully remove the jars and place them securely on a towel with at least an inch of space in between each jar. Let the jars cool down for 12 to 24 hours at room temperature.

To ensure that you destroy microorganisms in low-acid foods, process them in a pressure canner with the correct time and pressure corresponding to your altitude. If the temperature and time are incorrect, your food will spoil, resulting in wasted food and money. Thus, you should learn how to be accurate with the identification of the right temperature and time. A more thorough discussion on how to determine the processing time and pressure will be discussed in the next chapters. Different types of food will require different processing times and pressures. For instance, here is a table showing the recommended processing time and pressure for beef (National Institute of Food and Agriculture, n.d.).

Jar Size	Process Time	Canner Pressure According to Altitude			
		0-2,000 ft	2,001-4,000 ft	4,001-6,000 ft	6,001-8,000 ft
Pint	75 minutes	11 lb	12 lb	13 lb	14 lb
Quart	90 minutes	11 lb	12 lb	13 lb	14 lb

After processing your food and letting it cool for 12 to 24 hours, check if it is sealed properly to avoid food waste. You have three options to choose from when testing your jar seals. In general, you should remove the screw bands, then follow any of the three options below:

- Option 1: Using the bottom of a teaspoon, tap the lid of the jar. Observe if it produces a dull sound; this is an indication that it is not sealed. Meanwhile, if it is properly sealed, it will create a high-pitched ring.

- Option 2: Using a finger, press the middle of the lid to check if it springs up upon release. If it does, the lid does not seal properly.

- Option 3: Look across the lid as you hold the jar at eye level. Observe if the center of the lid is curved up or flat, as this indicates improper sealing. A safely sealed jar has a lid that is curved down slightly in the center.

Upon checking your jar, if it is not properly sealed, remove the lid and check if the sealing surface of the jar has any abrasion. If it has, change the jar, and the lid and reprocess it again within 24 hours. Yet, you may also opt to just freeze the processed foods instead of reprocessing them. You can consume frozen foods in improperly sealed jars within several days.

Preserving food through pressure canning is simple; all you have to do is follow the process and the recipe. The next important factor you should learn is how to focus on safety by properly following pressure canning procedures. After all, food safety has a significant effect on our health. Improper food processing may result in potential health hazards.

Chapter 4:

FOCUSING ON SAFETY

Food safety involves everybody in the food chain. –Mike Johanns

You have the responsibility to ensure that the food you and your family will eat is safe, especially now that you are the one who will process it. Correct and proper pressure canning will allow you to have great food that you can store at room temperature for a period of time. Ensuring food safety is a necessity for healthy living. Consuming improperly processed and handled food will put you and your family at risk. Thus, it is important to always practice safety precautions.

Common Pressure Canning Mistakes to Avoid

Mistakes are very easy to commit, especially for beginners. You are still building your knowledge of pressure canning, and you need every bit of help that is available. With food processing, you should always proceed with caution, as there are risks associated with improper food handling. Yet, you don't have to worry too much, as I have a list of common mistakes beginners make so that you don't commit the same mistakes. Even when I was using a pressure canner for the first time, I was very nervous. I don't want to end up being poisoned by the food I processed myself. Yet, I still managed to process a delicious mixed vegetable recipe without anything exploding. Along the way, I too, committed canning mistakes. However, none of those mistakes made me stop processing my own food.

Instead, it made me improve my food processing skills. Let me share with you some common beginner mistakes so you won't commit them, or you'll know how to remedy them:

- Overfilling your jars with food: You may be tempted to fill your jars up to the brim. However, as already discussed, you should always leave proper headspace. Your recipe will indicate how much headspace you should leave; it can range from half an inch to an inch. Headspace is important so that your self-sealing lid can seal the jar properly and for the jar to create enough vacuum. In addition, not leaving enough headspace will also result in the liquids inside the jar spilling over, further resulting in unsealed jars. Unsealed jars will force you to reprocess them or store them in the refrigerator to be consumed immediately. Be sure to leave enough headspace, as just one batch of unsealed jars can take up too much space in your refrigerator, and you will have too much food to consume in just a week. To make it easier for you to determine if you have enough headspace, use a canning funnel with headspace measurements.

- Reusing lids: Sometimes, we tend to become so economical and practical that we often reuse a lot of things. However, for safety purposes, I hope that you do not reuse your canning lids. Self-sealing lids are only meant for one pressure canning process. This is because the adhesive rubber on the underside of the lid wears out pretty fast. Reusing your lids will not guarantee properly sealed canned foods. If you want to reuse your lids, opt for reusable canning lids that have interchangeable rubber seals.

- Not cleaning the edges of the jar: It is necessary to wipe or clean the edges of the jar once it is already filled with food.

- Using jars without preheating: Your jars need to be preheated before filling them with foods and processing them in a pressure canner. Preheated jars help minimize siphoning or loss of liquid. Siphoning usually happens when extreme differences in temperature occur. Thus, to avoid this loss of liquid, your jars must already be hot before being put in the canner. In addition, extreme temperature differences can also result in jar breakage during processing. Aside from not preheating your jars, a more dangerous mistake you should avoid is putting cold jars in a pressure canner.

- Using jars with cracks or abrasions: Make it a habit to check all your canning jars for any abrasions, not just in the sealing area but also in the body of the jars. If you process food in a jar with a small abrasion, it will a most likely crack inside the pressure canner while processing. Just one small abrasion in a single jar can lead to a whole batch of canned foods being wasted. To avoid this, inspect the jars while you are washing them. Turn the jars one by one in your hand, check the rims for any chips, and inspect the sides for any cracks.

- Processing jars with air bubbles: Having air bubbles inside your jars means that there is air inside your jars. This can add more air to the headspace, which will make it hard for your jars to seal properly. In addition, the air trapped inside the jars will also make the food spoil, as the air gives bacteria the perfect environment to grow. Hence, you should always move a bubble popper or butter knife around the jar to help it release or burst air bubbles.

- Disturbing jars too early: After pressure canning your jars, you need to cool them down for 12 to 24 hours. Let the contents of the jar cool down, allowing the seal and vacuum to form properly. If you disturb the jars too early, the jars may not seal properly as the hot food comes into contact with the lid's adhesive part.

If you make a mistake, such as one that results in unsealed jars, reprocess the jars within 24 hours. If you notice unsealed jars after 24 hours, you need to throw them out already, or you may risk yourself or your family. However, if the foods that didn't process or seal well cannot handle reprocessing, such as green beans, freeze them instead and consume them within the week.

Essential Safety Tips to Keep In Mind

You can accomplish anything you set your mind to. Build the necessary skills that will allow you to master pressure canning. Don't worry too much, as everything can be learned. To help you become more prepared when pressure canning, here are some essential safety tips that will help you succeed in food processing:

- Use a pressure canner, not a pressure cooker: A pressure canner has a pressure gauge on it, while a pressure cooker only has a valve. For safe canning, be sure that what you have at home is a pressure canner and not a pressure cooker.

- Familiarize yourself with your pressure canner: Read the manual and instructions included in the box of your pressure canner so you will know how to properly operate it. Specifically, read about how much water you need to fill it, how to lock it, and how to operate it. You should also ensure that your pressure canner still has all of its parts. If there is any missing part, replace it before using it, especially if your canner has missing or broken locking mechanisms or gaskets.

- Properly follow recipes: You can be flexible or creative with your recipes. However, before you can do that, you need to learn the basics first. For instance, you should learn which ingredients you should not mix together and which ingredients you can substitute. After developing the necessary skills, you can then be creative with your recipes. In general, as a beginner, follow relevant recipes first, so you don't compromise your health.

- Use clean hands and equipment when handling food: Be sure to wash your hands with warm water and soap for about 20 seconds before you handle foods. When working with vegetables and fruits, wash them gently with cool, running, drinkable water before incorporating them in your recipe. When cutting your ingredients, use a different cutting board for produce and another board for raw meat, seafood, or poultry. Remember to sanitize your countertops before and after food preparations. Always clean during all phases of canning to avoid potential cross-contamination.

When processing your own food, always prioritize proper food handling. Your safety and health will greatly benefit if you practice safety precautions. You can start with easy-to-follow recipes as you develop your pressure canning skills. In the long run, you will surely enjoy the benefits of pressure canning, which will help you appreciate food sustainability campaigns.

Chapter 5:

BUILDING YOUR PREPPER PANTRY WITH PRESSURE-CANNED GOODS

Having a prepper pantry allows you to be prepared in case an emergency occurs. It lessens your stress, at least in terms of food sustainability, as you have easy access to healthy and enough food. For instance, whenever the inflation rate starts to rise, and foods start to get expensive pretty quickly, you won't have to worry too much as you have an adequate supply in your own home. In addition, since you are pressure canning your own foods at home, you will need a place to store your canned foods. It would be a waste if you didn't have proper storage for your canned foods, as they will spoil if improperly stored.

The Benefits of Having a Prepper's Pantry

It is beneficial to have your own pepper pantry. First, let us discuss what a pepper pantry is. It is simply a storage area for backup supplies, especially food. A pepper pantry is usually utilized to keep extra foods on hand whenever daily supplies run low. For instance, I appreciated having my own pepper pantry at home when home quarantine was implemented in 2020. People were discouraged from going out due to the dangers of getting infected with COVID-19. Luckily, I have a paper pantry full of foods I processed through pressure canning. With my variety of supplies, I was able to feed my family healthy and quality foods that were already available at home. Nobody in my family was forced to go out and compromise their health just to get supplies or panic-buy in crowded grocery stores where they could get infected. I am lucky that I have been pressure canning our foods and have prepared monthly meal plans for my family.

In general, a pepper pantry will allow everyone and anyone to get through any emergency or catastrophe. This is especially true for large families or families with dietary restrictions. During emergencies, it may be hard or expensive to access foods for a special diet. It would be nice to have foods fit for special dietary needs easily accessible to you in your prepper pantry. Being prepared during emergencies is crucial, as they are inevitable. Storms, hurricanes, pandemics, earthquakes, or even just power outages can happen from moment to moment. A prepper's pantry can really help ease the tension during such emergencies. Another event where a prepper pantry can be helpful is when the global economy comes down, and many companies implement massive layoffs of employees. While you may lose your job, at least you wouldn't have to worry about feeding your family and could expend your energy on looking for a new job.

A pepper pantry is significantly beneficial during emergencies, yet it can also be used for daily use. Take, for example, the situation where you were suddenly given so many projects at work that you barely had time to prepare food for your family. You can just easily get canned foods from your pantry and heat them for your dinner. Or if you forgot to get groceries due to a hectic day, at least when you get home, you have food stored in your pantry, ready to eat. Whatever your situation is, your future self will really thank you for being prepared for any future circumstances. With a prepper pantry, you can also start having family meal plans so your family gets the adequate nutrients needed to stay fit. Be sure to include your family members in building your prepper pantry so that everyone enjoys the food they consume. Having a well-maintained prepper pantry will also allow you to plan ahead. This means that you can prepare all the food you will eat for the month and just store it in your pantry. You won't have to cook every day; you just have to set aside one or two days a month for pressure canning.

Tips for Planning Your Prepper Pantry

There are a few things you need to consider when building your prepper pantry at home. To avoid having a stockpile that may just end up spoiling, you should have a strong organizational foundation. You just can't process too many pressure-canned foods and not eat them. You should have a plan for how you will consume them, too. In addition, you can't just stock food that your family doesn't even like eating. These foods will surely end up as food waste. To ensure that your prepper pantry becomes a useful part of your home, here are some tips that can help you:

- The first step is knowing your goals: This means that you need to identify the purpose of your prepper pantry. Is your prepper pantry for food security, peace of mind, building a community, or convenience? A prepper pantry for food security will allow you to have easy access to food whenever an unexpected situation occurs, such as a family member losing a steady supply of income or when the inflation rate increases. A prepper pantry for peace of mind simply allows you to ensure that you have food, just like you have insurance for your car and home. A prepper pantry aimed at building a community is one where you store food that you can give to people who need it at any time. Meanwhile, a prepper pantry for convenience allows you to have food to serve to your family without spending too much time cooking; this is especially beneficial when all of your family members are having hectic or busy days. Also, you don't have to wait for the appropriate time to consume your stored foods; you can consume your old stocks as a regular meal so they won't spoil. Just be sure that you have enough food for whatever your goal is in your prepper pantry. You can also have two prepper pantries—a working pantry and an emergency pantry:

- Working pantry: This is a pantry or cabinet full of foods for daily consumption. Most families have at least two to three months' worth of supplies in their working pantry. You don't have to buy or prepare all the foods at once. You can start small and build up your supply. Ensure that you have a variety of foods that can provide your family with the recommended daily intake of nutrients.

- Emergency pantry: The ideal emergency pantry must be established in a dry and clean part of your home. Preferably, your emergency pantry must be between 50–70° F and out of reach of pests. This pantry must only be accessed during emergencies, or you can rotate old items out of it before they spoil. Most households with an emergency pantry stock dried rice, beans, and pasta. There are households that have at least three months' worth of supplies, while some have years' worth.

- List food items you will need in a year or for how long you want your prepper pantry to last: You can't just add any food to your prepper pantry without a thought. It is recommended that you list down all the food items that your family eats in a year. Consider any food allergies and dietary restrictions. You should also account for the food favorites of each family member. After all, it would be nice to have access to food that you enjoy even in emergencies; it can lessen the tension. It may be overwhelming to list these food items. Thus, it would be helpful to just recall what you and your family have eaten for the past month and just multiply it by 12, or for how many months worth of food you wish to store. Make sure that you have a good variety of foods, accounting for adequate and healthy amounts of carbohydrates, protein, fats, and other micronutrients.

- Plan your meals: To make it easier to decide which foods to store, you can plan your meals. You can either do it per week or per month. Just make sure that you have enough rotation and variety, as it is not enjoyable to eat the same variety of foods over and over again. After planning your meals, you will need to determine the amount of food your family needs. Take into consideration how much food per meal all members need. An easy way to do this is to calculate the daily or weekly caloric needs of each individual, and then you can determine how much food to store per day or week. Meal planning will also allow you to save money, as buying foods in bulk is more cost-effective. Yet, you should keep in mind that meal planning will require recipes. Your recipes will tell you how much of each ingredient you should buy, as well as how many ingredients each jar will require when pressure canning. Another thing you should note is the need to label each jar by processed date and recipe name.

- Label the nutrient value of each food you store: If you are following a recipe, the nutrient content of the food is usually written in the recipe. It would be helpful to write it down on the jar label too. You can also keep a record of the nutrient content in your meal plan so you can ensure that each member gets the recommended daily intake of micronutrients needed by their body. Aside from looking at the nutrient content, you should also take note of each member's comfort food. Just make sure that you have a balance of healthy food and comfort food. Your family should not just live off junk food during emergencies, as it can worsen your living conditions. Living in emergencies may also require people to do manual work, especially when the electricity is down; hence, you should prepare meals with high-energy foods, such as beans and nuts, and hearty grains in your prepper pantry.

- Consider the space where you will establish your prepper pantry: The space in your prepper pantry must accommodate the amount of food you want to store. For instance, if you only have a limited amount of space for your prepper pantry, you will most likely not be able to store a year's supply of food. Yet, you can also get creative with your prepper pantry area. You can look for any unused area in your house, such as under the stairs, as long as it is not accessible to any pests. You may also create a space for your pantry by dividing a large room into two, making room for shelves of pantry foods. Having shelves in your prepper pantry will also make it easier to rotate your food supplies. It can also make your pantry more organized, as you can have a dedicated shelf area for each food type, or you may also store your food by the date it is processed.

- Track your inventory: Tracking your inventory will allow you to determine how much food you already have and how much more you need. In addition, your tracker must include the nutritional value and the processing date of your inventory. With this, you will know if your stock is enough for your family's nutritional and caloric needs. You will also know if there are food items you need to rotate out of your emergency pantry, such as foods that were processed more than a year ago. It would be easy if you tracked your inventory either on graph paper or in an Excel file.

- Ensure that your pantry is safe from pests: Be sure to have a regular inspection of your pantry to see if there are any pests living in it. This is especially true if you have flour and grains in your pantry. You can also invest in rodent repellents; just ensure that they are out of reach of small children and pets. Always check if your food supplies are sealed in airtight and sturdy containers. Be sure that there are spaces between jars or supplies for easier inspection and management.

Now that you know how to establish and maintain a prepper pantry, let us discuss how to store your canned foods. Usually, canned foods can last for a year, although some can remain consumable for a longer period. When storing your canned foods, always remember to keep them in a cool, dry place away from sunlight. Be sure that each jar has a label with the recipe name and date processed. Avoid storage areas that are damp, as it can corrode metal lids, leading to unsealed jars. Before consumption, always check for any mold, discoloration, or bad smell. If you observe such behavior, discard your canned foods immediately. For safety purposes, here are some ways to thoroughly examine jars:

- Examine the tightness and seal of the lids. As discussed, sealed lids have concave centers.

- Observe the jars at eye level to see if there are streaks of dried food at the top of the jars.

- Check the contents of the jar for any unnatural colors or air bubbles.

- Upon opening the jar, observe if there is any spurting liquid, cotton-like mold, or an unnatural smell.

All About Meal Planning and How to Start

Meal planning will keep you on track, especially on days when you barely have time for meal preparation. Your meal plan will also dictate which foods and recipes you will process through pressure canning. In addition, it is also associated with a healthier lifestyle and a balanced diet, as it allows you to consider your daily nutrient and caloric needs. Meal planning may sound complicated, but it is actually pretty simple, and all you have to do is decide what you will eat for the next few days or for the week. In terms of your prepper pantry, you can also decide what you will eat weekly during emergencies.

To help you start with your very own meal plans, here are some considerations:

- Select appropriate recipes: When doing this, consider your budget and skill level. You may also start by determining which ingredients you have. For instance, if you have a garden, determine which of your crops are ready for harvest. Then, you can start looking for recipes that you can put together using your harvest as ingredients. Another consideration is the available time you have for food processing. It would be helpful if you asked your family members what foods they wanted to eat for the week or month. Outright, asking your family what they want to eat will help save time compared to doing all the thinking yourself. It would also make your family members feel more involved in household chores and meal planning. In fact, you can also encourage and empower them to help with actual food processing.

- Make a shopping list or list of ingredients: If your chosen recipe has ingredients you don't already have, then make a list of everything you need. You can save money if you buy in bulk. Since you are pressure canning, you can store your recipes for a long period of time; hence, it is efficient if you cook a number of jars of the same food so you can save money. Hence, for cost-effectiveness, plan your meals for a month or two. However, if you are just beginning to learn pressure canning, start small. Write down everything you need, including the quantities. It is also cost-effective to study which ingredients you can substitute. For instance, if a recipe requires quinoa, which you don't have, you can substitute it with brown rice, provided that you already have brown rice. Be sure that after getting back from shopping, you prep the food immediately. This will make cooking faster and easier.

- Prepare meals: Meal planning will require you to actually prepare your meals. It is time-efficient to cook your meals in batches. For instance, if you have a large pressure canner, you can cook four quart-jars of protein-rich meals that your family can eat for four meals. After that, you can choose to cook another batch of vegetables for your family's fiber needs for the week. Be sure that you know how much time you can spend on meal preparation.

- Create a journal of your recipes: You can search for online recipes or follow recipes written in this book. Whatever recipe you use, just make sure that you record it by writing it down or saving it on your computer. This will help you remake any recipe that you or your family enjoyed eating. As your skill grows, you may tweak some of the ingredients, such as making it low-sodium. It is also helpful to create a meal journal where you can write down what meals you have eaten every day. This will help you look back on what you can cook easily and which foods your family enjoyed. You will also remember which recipes you have not eaten for a while and which ones you have been eating from time to time so you can determine the right variety of foods to prepare next.

- Make it a habit: Make this a habit so you can fully reap the benefits of meal planning and pressure canning. You can do this by incorporating food processing into your schedule. For instance, you can allot one day a week or a month to cook batches of canned foods. Then, after a few weeks or months of doing this, you will know which recipes are more efficient to cook and which foods your family enjoys eating. Then, your meal plans will improve as time passes. Slowly, this habit will allow you to fill your prepper pantry—both your working and emergency pantry.

- Make a schedule: This will require you to start a calendar where you will list what you will eat per meal per day. In addition, your calendar can also remind you of any upcoming birthdays of your family members, so you can prepare any food you want to serve in advance. In addition, you may also set theme nights or days. For instance, for the month of January, every Monday is fish night, every Tuesday is pasta night, and so on. You can get as creative as you like while making sure that your family enjoys every meal. Do not forget to include it in your shopping and prep days. Take note of when and what products are on sale in your local grocery stores and adjust your shopping schedule accordingly.

When it comes to building your prepper pantry, start small. Begin by learning easy pressure canning recipes, then expand to more complicated ones as your skills improve. It is also recommended that you include your storage area in your meal planning, as you will only waste foods if you have no proper storage plans for them.

For more ideas, here are some prepper pantry products that some households have at home:

- rice, grains, and pasta

- canned vegetables

- canned meats, poultry, and seafood

- canned or dried beans

- peanut butter

- items for baking

- canned soups

- nuts and seeds

- pasta sauces and other sauces

- staples like oil, vinegar, and soy sauce

Now that you know how to process foods through pressure canning and how to store them in a prepper pantry, you are ready to learn pressure canning recipes. As long as you follow safety precautions and recipes, you will surely reap the benefits of pressure canning. Just remember to start small and take every process as a learning opportunity.

Chapter 6:

RECIPES FOR PRESSURE CANNING MEATS

Pressure canning is essential for preserving meats, as these are low-acid foods that require special care to prevent the growth of harmful bacteria.

Water bath canning is not sufficient for meat, due to its low acidity. To help you get started on pressure canning meats safely and effectively, here are some expert tips:

Why Pressure Canning for Meats is Important

Meats are low-acid foods, which means they require special food processing methods. **Water bathing alone won't kill harmful bacteria in meat**, so pressure canning is the recommended method to ensure your canned meats are safe and long-lasting.

Safety First: Considerations for Meat Canning

It's important to be extra cautious when processing meat. Unlike fruits and vegetables, **meat lacks the necessary acidity to naturally kill bacteria**. A poorly processed jar could pose a health risk to you and your family, so always adhere to safety guidelines.

5 Essential Tips for Pressure Canning Meats

1. **Use High-Quality, Chilled Meat**: Always start with meat that is fresh and has been properly chilled. Poor quality meat can compromise the safety and taste of your final product.

2. **Debone the Meat: Remove any large bones** from the meat prior to canning. This not only makes for easier packing but also ensures thorough cooking during the pressure canning process.

3. **Trim Excess Fat**: **Remove any excess fat** before canning. While it's generally safe, the fat will rise to the top and may affect the food's appearance.

4. **Form Ground Meat**: If you're canning ground meat, feel free to form it into balls or patties. Just make sure to **avoid adding flour, eggs, or rice**, as these ingredients could affect the canning process.

5. **Start with Trusted Recipes**: Especially if you are a beginner, **stick with recipes that have been tested and proven safe** for pressure canning.

Remember, pressure canning meat is not difficult but it does require careful attention to detail to ensure safety. Always follow trusted recipes and guidelines.

Pressure Canning Beef: A Comprehensive Guide

Storing pressure-canned beef provides you with ready-to-serve, delicious meat for those days when you can't spend hours in the kitchen.

Whether your beef is ground, cubed, or in strips, pressure canning offers a safe and efficient way to preserve it. Below is a detailed guide on how to can beef using both hot-pack and raw pack methods.

Why Pressure Canning Beef is Beneficial

Having a stockpile of canned beef ensures a **quick and easy dinner option**. The beef becomes tender and flavorful, making it a perfect addition to various meals.

General Guidelines for Canning Beef

Regardless of the cut, **removing excess fat** is crucial. This is true whether you are hot-packing or raw-packing the beef.

Hot-Pack vs Raw-Pack: What's the Difference?

1. **Hot-Pack Method**

   - **Precook the Beef**: Cook it until it's rare, using methods like stewing, roasting, or browning in a small amount of fat.

- **Jar Filling**: Once cooked, fill the beef into your canning jars. Cover them with a liquid (water, broth, or tomato juice), leaving a **one-inch headspace**.

2. **Raw-Pack Method**

- **Jar Filling**: Simply place small cuts or chunks of raw beef into the canning jars, leaving a **one-inch headspace**.

- **No Need for Extra Liquid**: The beef will release its own juices during the pressure canning process.

Canning Process: Key Considerations

- **Temperature Control**: Ensure the canner is preheated appropriately. For raw-packing, preheat to 140°F; for hot-packing, aim for 180°F. Proper preheating prevents drastic temperature changes, which could lead to jar breakage.

Recommended Processing Times and Pressures for Chunks of Beef

Type of Canner	Jar Size	Process Time (in minutes)	Canner Pressure (in lb)				
			0–1,000 ft	1,001–2,000 ft	2,001–4,000 ft	4,001–6,000 ft	6,001–8,000 ft
Dial Gauge	Pint	75	11		12	13	14
	Quart	90	11		12	13	14
Weighted Gauge	Pint	75	10	15			
	Quart	90	10	15			

Note for Ground Beef

38

For ground beef, only hot packing is possible. You must precook the meat to render out fat and set its shape. The processing time and pressure for ground beef are similar to those for beef chunks.

Now that you know how to pressure can beef, here are some recipes for you to try:

BEEF POT ROAST

Time: 2 hours and 30 minutes

Serving Size: 1 pint-jar (1 lb beef) or 1 quart-jar (2 lbs beef)

Prep Time: 1 hour

Processing Time: [Time required in the pressure canner, not specified in original recipe]

Cook Time: 1 hour and 30 minutes

Description

Pot roast is an American classic made from tougher cuts of beef. This beginner-friendly recipe only requires three ingredients and uses the hot packing method. Perfect for anyone new to pressure canning!

Ingredients:

- 500g or 1 lb beef round for 1 pint-jar; or 1 kg or 2 lbs for 1 quart-jar
- Pickling salt (optional)
- Water (can be substituted with stock or tomato juice)

Tools Needed:

- Pressure canner
- Canning jars with lids and rings
- Skillet
- Funnel
- Jar lifter
- Ladle
- Bubble popper or butter knife

Directions:

1. **Prepare Beef**: Cut off the gristle or cartilage from your beef round, and then cut it into cubes or strips that can fit into the mouth of your canning jars.

2. **Brown Beef**: In a skillet, heat a small amount of fat or oil to brown the beef. Make sure all sides are seared to a rare color.

3. **Pack Jars**: Pack the browned beef into your canning jars, leaving a one-inch headspace.

4. **Add Salt**: Optionally, add 1/2 teaspoon of pickling salt per pint jar or 1 teaspoon per quart jar.

5. **Add Liquid**: Fill jars with hot water, stock, or tomato juice, maintaining a one-inch headspace.

6. **Debubble**: Use a bubble popper or butter knife to remove air bubbles from the jar.

7. **Seal and Process**: Wipe jar rims, place lids, and process in a pressure canner according to the manufacturer's guidelines and your altitude.

Notes:

- The nutrition facts are calculated per serving of 100g with salt.

Nutrition Facts per 100g Serving

Nutrition Component	Amount
Calories	94 kcal
Calories from fat	16
Total fat	1.8 g
Saturated fat	0.6 g
Sodium	59 mg
Cholesterol	29 mg
Protein	18.8 g

BEEF SHORT RIB

Time: 2 hours and 30 minutes

Serving Size: 1 pint-jar (500g of rib) or 1 quart-jar (1 kg of rib)

Prep Time: 1 hour

Processing Time: [Time required in the pressure canner, not specified in original recipe]

Cook Time: 1 hour and 30 minutes

Description:

Beef Short Rib is another American classic, similar to pot roast but using beef short rib as the main ingredient. This beginner-friendly recipe involves just three simple ingredients and yields a delicious outcome.

Ingredients:

- 500g of beef short rib for 1 pint-jar; or 1 kg for 1 quart-jar
- Pickling salt (optional)
- Water (can be substituted with tomato juice or stock)

Tools Needed:

- Pressure canner
- Canning jars with lids and rings
- Skillet
- Funnel
- Jar lifter
- Ladle
- Bubble popper or butter knife

Directions:

1. **Prepare the Ribs**: Cut the beef short ribs into chunks that will fit the mouth of your canning jars. You may leave the small bones in.
2. **Brown the Ribs**: In a skillet, heat a small amount of fat or oil to brown the rib chunks. If browning in batches, keep the already browned chunks in a covered pot to keep them hot.
3. **Pack the Jars**: Pack the browned rib chunks into your canning jars, leaving a one-inch headspace.
4. **Optional Salt**: Add 1/2 teaspoon of pickling salt for pint jars or 1 teaspoon for quart jars. You may also use other non-clouding salts.
5. **Add Liquid**: Fill the jars with hot water, stock, or tomato juice, ensuring a one-inch headspace remains.

6. **Debubble and Seal**: Wipe the jar rims clean and use a bubble popper or butter knife to remove air bubbles. Then place the lids on the jars.
7. **Process**: Follow manufacturer's guidelines and altitude table for pressure. Start the timer once the recommended pressure is reached.

Notes:

- Please specify the processing time according to your pressure canner and altitude for safety.

Nutrition Facts per 100g Serving:

Nutrition Component	Amount
Calories	205 kcal
Calories from fat	81
Total fat	9 g
Saturated fat	3.4 g
Sodium	60 mg
Cholesterol	91 mg
Protein	28.9 g

PRESSURE CANNING PORK: YOUR COMPLETE GUIDE

Whether you're dealing with chunks or ground pork, the pressure canning process is fairly similar to that of beef. Having canned pork on hand ensures that you always have a quick, tasty, and protein-rich meal option. This comprehensive guide covers everything you need to know, from the type of meat to use to the exact processing times and pressures.

Essential Considerations for Canning Pork

Just like with beef, **high-quality, chilled pork** is the way to go. Pork has more fat than beef, so it's even more important to **remove excess fat** before canning.

Hot-Pack vs Raw-Pack: What's the Difference?

1. **Hot-Pack Method**

   - This is the **recommended** method for ground pork.

   - **Precook the Pork**: Similar to beef, the meat should be cooked until rare.

   - **Jar Filling**: Place the precooked pork into canning jars and cover with liquid, leaving a **one-inch headspace**.

2. **Raw-Pack Method**

   - **Jar Filling**: Simply pack chunks of raw pork into your canning jars, also leaving a **one-inch headspace**.

   - **Natural Juices**: No additional liquid is necessary, as the pork will release its own juices during the canning process.

Processing Time and Pressure

The processing times and pressures are almost identical to those for beef. However, pork might require different seasonings due to its distinct flavor.

Type of Canner	Jar Size	Process Time (in minutes)	Canner Pressure (in lb)				
			0–1,000 ft	1,001–2,000 ft	2,001–4,000 ft	4,001–6,000 ft	6,001–8,000 ft
Dial Gauge	Pint	75	11		12	13	14
	Quart	90	11		12	13	14
Weighted Gauge	Pint	75	10	15			
	Quart	90	10	15			

Beginner-Friendly Pork Recipes

There are a plethora of pork recipes suitable for pressure canning. Whether you're interested in canning pulled pork, pork chili, or simple pork chunks, the options are limitless.

Equipped with this guide, you're now ready to embark on your pressure canning journey with pork. Happy canning!

PRESSURE-CANNED PORK

Time: 2 hours and 30 minutes

Serving Size: 1 pint-jar (500g of pork) or 1 quart-jar (1 kg of pork)

Prep Time: 1 hour

Processing Time: Refer to Pressure Canning Guidelines

Cook Time: 1 hour and 30 minutes

Description:

This simple American main course features any cut of pork, as long as it doesn't contain large bones. It is a beginner-friendly recipe that calls for only three basic ingredients.

Ingredients:

- 500g of pork for a pint-jar; or 1 kg for a quart-jar
- Pickling salt (optional, 0.5 tablespoon for pint or 1 tablespoon for quart)
- Water (can be substituted with tomato juice or beef broth/stock)

Tools Needed:

- Pressure canner
- Canning jars with lids and rings
- Skillet
- Funnel
- Jar lifter
- Ladle
- Bubble popper or butter knife

Directions:

1. **Prepare Pork**: Remove large bones, excess fat, and gristle or cartilage. Cut the pork into chunks that will fit in your canning jars.
2. **Brown Pork**: In a skillet, heat a small amount of fat or oil to brown the pork chunks. If browning in batches, keep the browned chunks in a covered pot to keep them hot.

3. **Pack Jars**: Transfer the browned pork into your canning jars, leaving a one-inch headspace.
4. **Optional Seasoning**: Add pickling salt to taste. Other types of salt or spices like oregano, onion powder, or paprika can also be used.
5. **Add Liquid**: Fill the jars with hot liquid—either water, beef broth, or tomato juice—ensuring a one-inch headspace remains.
6. **Debubble and Seal**: Wipe the rims clean and debubble the jars using a bubble popper or butter knife. Place the lids on the jars.
7. **Process**: Follow the Pressure Canning Guidelines for the pressure settings based on your altitude. Start your timer once the recommended pressure is reached.

Notes:

- Please consult the Pressure Canning Guidelines table for accurate processing times based on your altitude and type of canner for safety.

Nutrition Facts per 100g Serving:

Nutrition Component	Amount
Calories	263 kcal
Saturated fat	8 g
Sodium	61 mg
Cholesterol	72 mg
Protein	17 g
Potassium	287 mg
Iron	1 mg

PULLED PORK

Time: 1 hour and 50 minutes

Serving Size: 1 pint-jar (500g of pork) or 1 quart-jar (1 kg of pork)

Prep Time: 20 minutes

Processing Time: Refer to Pressure Canning Guidelines

Cook Time: 1 hour and 30 minutes

Description:

Pressure-canned pulled pork is a versatile main dish that pairs well with many recipes. This beginner-friendly recipe features pork butt and can be flavored with barbecue sauce.

Ingredients:

- Pork butt (500 g for a pint-jar; or 1 kg for a quart-jar)
- Barbecue sauce (optional, 1/4 cup for pint-jar; or 1 cup for quart-jar)
- Water or beef stock

Tools Needed:

- Pressure canner
- Canning jars with lids and rings
- Funnel
- Jar lifter
- Ladle
- Bubble popper or butter knife

Directions:

1. **Prepare Pork**: Shred the pre-tenderized pork butt. Pack the shredded pork into your canning jars, leaving a one-inch headspace.
2. **Add Sauce and Liquid**: For a pint-jar, add 1/4 cup of hot barbecue sauce. Fill the jar with hot water or beef stock until a one-inch headspace is reached. You can opt out of using barbecue sauce if desired.
3. **Debubble and Seal**: Wipe the rims clean and debubble the jars using a bubble popper or butter knife. Seal the jars with the lids.

4. **Process**: Follow the Pressure Canning Guidelines for pressure settings based on your altitude. Start the timer when the recommended pressure is reached.

Notes:

- The Preparation Time does not account for the time needed to tenderize the pork butt.
- Please consult the Pressure Canning Guidelines table for accurate processing times based on your altitude and type of canner for safety.

Nutrition Facts per 100g Serving:

Nutrition Component	Amount
Calories	194 kcal
Total fat	6.2 g
Saturated fat	2 g
Total carbohydrate	4.5 g
Sodium	191 mg
Cholesterol	83 mg
Protein	28.2 g
Potassium	368 mg
Iron	1 mg

PRESSURE CANNING CHICKEN: YOUR COMPREHENSIVE GUIDE

Canning chicken can be a convenient way to store protein for quick meals. However, the process for chicken is a bit different than that for beef and pork, both in terms of preparation and canning pressures. This guide will walk you through each step.

Preparation Tips for Canning Chicken

1. **Freshly Killed and Dressed**: Ideally, use chicken that has been freshly killed and dressed.

2. **Chilling**: Chill dressed chicken for 6 to 12 hours before canning.

3. **Cutting**: Cut the chicken into pieces small enough to fit the mouth of your canning jars.

4. **Fat Removal**: Like beef and pork, be sure to **remove excess fat** from the chicken.

5. **Bone-in vs. Boneless**: Chicken can be canned with or without bones.

Hot-Pack vs Raw-Pack Methods

1. **Hot-Pack Method**

   - **Partial Cooking**: Bake, boil, or steam the chicken until it is about 2/3 done.

   - **Jar Filling**: Pack the partially cooked chicken into jars and cover with hot liquid.

   - **Headspace**: Leave **one and 1/4 inches** of headspace.

2. **Raw-Pack Method**

   - **Jar Filling**: Simply fill the jars with raw, cut chicken.

   - **Headspace**: Similarly, leave **one and 1/4 inches** of headspace.

Processing Time and Pressure for Chicken

Differences in processing times and pressures exist depending on whether your chicken is bone-in or boneless.

Chicken Without Bones

Type of Canner	Jar Size	Process Time (in minutes)	Canner Pressure (in lb)				
			0–1,000 ft	1,001– 2,000 ft	2,001– 4,000 ft	4,001- 6,000 ft	6,001– 8,000 ft
Dial Gauge	Pint	75	11		12	13	14
	Quart	90	11		12	13	14
Weighted Gauge	Pint	75	10	15			
	Quart	90	10	15			

Chicken With Bones

Type of Canner	Jar Size	Process Time (in minutes)	Canner Pressure (in lb)				
			0–1,000 ft	1,001– 2,000 ft	2,001— 4,000 ft	4,001– 6,000 ft	6,001– 8,000 ft
Dial Gauge	Pint	65	11		12	13	14
	Quart	75	11		12	13	14
	Pint	65	10	15			

Weighted Gauge	Quart	75	10	15

Beginner-Friendly Chicken Recipes

Once you have all the basics down, it's time to experiment with various chicken recipes suitable for pressure canning. From chicken soups and stews to chicken casseroles, the possibilities are endless.

With this guide at your side, you're well-prepared to start your pressure canning journey with chicken. Happy canning!

CANNED CHICKEN AND GRAVY

Time: 2 hours

Serving Size: Two quart-jars

Prep Time: 30 minutes

Processing Time: Refer to Pressure Canning Guidelines

Cook Time: 1 hour and 30 minutes

Description:

This American main course dish serves as a complete meal in a jar. You can pour it over rice or potatoes after heating and thickening. Although the name states "gravy," you make the gravy upon opening the jar. The recipe uses the raw packing method.

Ingredients:

- One kg boneless chicken
- Chicken stock or water
- Onion (about 175 g)
- Potato (about 175 g)
- Celery (about 175 g)
- Salt (two teaspoons)
- Ground black pepper (one teaspoon)
- White wine (four tablespoons)

Tools Needed:

- Pressure canner
- Two quart-size canning jars with lids and rings
- Chopping board and knife
- Mixing bowl
- Ladle

- Bubble popper or butter knife

Directions:

1. **Prepare Ingredients**: Wash and peel the onion, celery, and potato. Chop or dice them. Cut the chicken into chunks that will fit into your canning jars. Combine all these ingredients in a bowl (excluding chicken stock or water).

2. **Fill Jars**: Load your canning jars with the mixture, ensuring to leave a 1 and 1/4-inch headspace.

3. **Add Liquid**: Pour in chicken broth or water over the mixture, keeping the same headspace.

4. **Debubble and Clean**: Before sealing, debubble the jars and wipe the rims clean.

5. **Process**: Follow the Pressure Canning Guidelines for boneless chicken. Start your timer once you hit the recommended pressure.

Notes:

- Please consult the Pressure Canning Guidelines table for accurate processing times based on your altitude and type of canner for safety.

Nutrition Facts per 100g Serving:

Nutrition Component	Amount
Calories	158 kcal
Total fat	3 g
Saturated fat	1 g
Total carbohydrate	6 g
Sodium	836 mg
Cholesterol	61 mg
Protein	25 g
Fiber	1 g
Sugar	1 mg

CANNED CHICKEN RECIPE

Time: 2 hours 30 minutes

Serving Size: Varies (500 g for a pint jar or one kg for a quart jar)

Prep Time: 1 hour

Processing Time: Refer to Pressure Canning Guidelines

Cook Time: 1 hour and 30 minutes

Description:

This easier, beginner-friendly recipe requires just three ingredients. The chicken can be used in various quick meal recipes later on. The method used here is hot packing.

Ingredients:

- Chicken (500 g for a pint jar or one kg for a quart jar)
- Chicken broth
- Salt

Tools Needed:

- Pressure canner
- Canning jars with lids and rings (pint or quart size)
- Chopping board and knife
- Skillet
- Ladle
- Bubble popper or butter knife

Directions:

1. **Prepare Chicken**: Use any chicken parts you prefer, either with or without bones, and with or without skin. Cut the chicken into sizes that will fit the canning jars.

2. **Brown Chicken**: Brown the chicken so it's about 2/3 cooked. Transfer the partially cooked chicken into your canning jars, leaving a 1 and 1/4-inch headspace.

3. **Add Broth**: Pour hot chicken broth or water into the jars, maintaining the same headspace.

4. **Debubble and Clean**: Before sealing, debubble the jars and wipe the rims clean.

5. **Process**: Follow the Pressure Canning Guidelines based on your altitude and the type of chicken you are using. Start your timer once you reach the recommended pressure.

Notes:

- Consult the Pressure Canning Guidelines table for processing times and pressures based on your altitude and whether you're using chicken with or without bones.

Nutrition Facts per 100g Serving:

Nutrition Component	Amount
Calories	153 kcal
Total fat	3.1 g
Saturated fat	0.9 g
Total carbohydrate	0.2 g
Sodium	247 mg
Cholesterol	77 mg
Protein	29.1 g
Calcium	16 mg
Potassium	190 mg
Iron	1 mg

PRESSURE CANNING FISH AND TUNA

Pressure canning fish and tune offers a great way to preserve these high-protein foods for later use.

However, canning fish can be more complex compared to beef, pork, or chicken due to its unique characteristics and food safety considerations. This guide provides an in-depth look at how to properly pressure can fish and tuna.

Canning Fish in Pint Jars

Fish Types and Preparation

- Suitable for **salmon, mackerel, steelhead, bluefish, trout**, and other fatty fish except tuna.

- **Bleed and eviscerate** within 2 hours of catching.

- **Chill** the cleaned fish on ice until canning.

- **Rinse** with cold water; add vinegar to remove slime.

- **Cut and Clean**: Remove fins, tails, and heads; cut into 3 1/2-inch pieces.

Canning Steps

1. Pack the fish into **preheated pint jars**.

2. Optional: Add **one teaspoon of salt** per jar.

3. **Don't add liquid.**

4. Leave **one inch of headspace**.

Recommended Processing Times for Pint Jars

Type of Canner	Jar Size		Canner Pressure (in lb)

		Process Time (in minutes)	0–1,000 ft	1,001–2,000 ft	2,001–4,000 ft	4,001–6,000 ft	6,001–8,000 ft
Dial Gauge	Pint	100	11		12	13	14
Weighted Gauge	Pint	100	10	15			

Canning Fish in Quart Jars

Preparation

- Similar to pint jars.

- **Vent for 10 minutes** after the steam starts.

- **Minimum of 160 minutes of processing** at the recommended pressure is required.

Recommended Processing Times for Quart Jars

Type of Canner	Jar Size	Process Time (in minutes)	Canner Pressure (in lb)				
			0–1,000 ft	1,001–2,000 ft	2,001–4,000 ft	4,001–6,000 ft	6,001–8,000 ft
Dial Gauge	Pint	160	11		12	13	14
Weighted Gauge	Pint	160	10	15			

TUNA

Preparation

- **Clean** and **drain** the blood.

- **Precook**: In an oven or steamer.

- **Refrigerate overnight**.

- **Peel skin**, remove vessels and discoloration, and debone.

Canning Steps

1. **Cut** and **pack** the tuna in jars.

2. **Add water or oil**; optional salt.

3. Leave **one inch of headspace**.

Recommended Processing Times for Tuna

Type of Canner	Jar Size	Process Time (in minutes)	Canner Pressure (in lb)				
			0–1,000 ft	1,001– 2,000 ft	2,001– 4,000 ft	4,001– 6,000 ft	6,001– 8,000 ft
Dial Gauge	Pint	100	11		12	13	14
Weighted Gauge	Pint	100	10	15			

Processing meat is easy. Just start small and use simple, beginner-friendly recipes. As your skills develop, you can opt for more complicated recipes. For now, enjoy the process and build the habit of pressure canning your own meals. In the next chapter, you will be provided with guidelines and recipes for pressure canning vegetables.

Chapter 7:

RECIPES FOR PRESSURE CANNING VEGETABLES

Most vegetables are low-acid foods. This means that it is necessary to process them through pressure canning to ensure that botulism and other harmful bacteria are killed. There are various vegetables, and each of them has unique preparation and processing methods. In this chapter, you will be provided with pressure canning recipes for some common vegetables. For a beginner, you will begin learning easy-to-follow vegetable recipes. From that foundation, you can expand your knowledge and be ready for pressure canning other complicated vegetable recipes. For now, here are some recipes that are staples in most households.

CARROTS

Time: Varies

Serving Size: Varies

Prep Time: Varies

Processing Time: 25-30 minutes

Cook Time: 5 minutes (for hot pack)

Description:

A beginner-friendly recipe for preserving carrots, perfect for use in quick recipes. Store them for months without worrying about spoilage.

Ingredients:

- Carrots without tops (about 1 kg per quart)

- Optional: Salt (1 teaspoon per quart)

Tools Needed:

- Pressure canner

- Canning jars with lids and rings (pint or quart size)

- Pot for boiling (if hot packing)

- Chopping board and knife

- Ladle

- Bubble popper or butter knife

Directions:

1. **Wash and Peel**: Clean the carrots thoroughly and peel them. Wash again and slice or dice as desired.

2. **Packing Method**: Choose between a hot pack or a raw pack. For hot packing, simmer the carrots in boiling water for 5 minutes.

3. **Fill Jars**: Load the preheated canning jars with carrots, maintaining an inch of headspace. Optionally, add 1 teaspoon of salt per quart. Fill with hot water or cooking liquid.

4. **Debubble and Clean**: Remove air bubbles and clean the jar rims. Seal the jars with lids.

Pressure Canning Guidelines:

To process your carrots inside the pressure canner, here are the recommended processing times and pressures (National Institute for Food and Agriculture, n.d.):

Type of Canner	Jar Size	Process Time (in minutes)	Canner Pressure (in lb)				
			0–1,000 ft	1,001–2,000 ft	2,001–4,000 ft	4,001–6,000 ft	6,001–8,000 ft
Dial Gauge	Pint	25	11		12	13	14
	Quart	30	11		12	13	14
Weighted Gauge	Pint	25	10	15			
	Quart	30	10	15			

Nutrition Facts (Per 100g Serving)

Nutrient	Amount
Calories	41 kcal
Total Fat	0 g
Saturated Fat	0 g
Carbohydrates	9.8 g
Total Sugars	4.9 g

Nutrient	Amount
Sodium	301 mg
Cholesterol	0 mg
Protein	0.8 g
Calcium	33 mg
Potassium	320 mg
Iron	0 mg

CORN CREAM-STYLE RECIPE

Skill Level: Beginner

Special Equipment: Pressure Canner

Safety Considerations:

- Take extra caution to debubble jars to remove trapped air.

- Ensure that jar rims are clean for a secure seal.

Ingredients:

- Corn on the cob (1 kg per pint)

- Salt (half a teaspoon per pint)

- Water

Instructions:

1. Preparation: Remove the husk and the silk from the corn. Wash the ears.

2. Blanching: Blanch the ears of corn for about four minutes.

3. Cutting: Cut off the corn kernels from the cob and scrape to release the "cream."

4. Cooking: Place corn in a saucepan, add boiling water and salt. Bring to a boil.

5. Jar Filling: Fill your preheated canning jars with the mixture, leaving a one-inch headspace.

6. Sealing: Debubble jars, clean the rims, and adjust the lids.

Pressure Canning Information:

Here are the recommended processing times and pressures for the corn cream-style recipe:

	Jar Size		

Type of Canner		Process Time (in minutes)	Canner Pressure (in lb)				
			0–1,000 ft	1,001–2,000 ft	2,001–4,000 ft	4,001–6,000 ft	6,001–8,000 ft
Dial Gauge	Pint	85	11		12	13	14
Weighted Gauge	Pint	85	10	15			

Nutrition Facts (per 100g serving):

Nutrient	Amount
Calories	1 kcal
Total Fat	0 g
Saturated Fat	0 g
Carbohydrates	0.3 g
Total Sugars	0.1 g
Sodium	233 mg
Cholesterol	0 mg
Protein	0.1 g
Calcium	0 mg
Potassium	4 mg
Iron	0 mg

WHOLE CORN KERNELS RECIPE

Skill Level: Beginner

Special Equipment: Pressure Canner

Safety Considerations:

- Take extra caution to debubble jars to remove trapped air.

- Ensure that jar rims are clean for a secure seal.

Ingredients:

- Corn on the cob (1 kg per pint or 2 kg per quart)

- Water or other cooking liquid

Instructions:

1. **Preparation**: Remove the husk and silk and wash the corn ears. Blanch for 3 minutes.

2. **Cutting**: Cut the kernels at about 3/4 depth. Do not scrape the cob.

3. **Packing Methods**:

   - **Hot Pack**: Place kernels in a saucepan with boiling water. Simmer for about 5 minutes. Add to preheated jars.

   - **Raw Pack**: Fill preheated jars with raw kernels and add cooking liquid. Optionally, add salt.

4. **Sealing**: Debubble jars and clean the rims. Adjust lids and process in a pressure canner.

Pressure Canning Information:

Type of Canner	Jar Size		Canner Pressure (in lb)

		Process Time (in minutes)	0–1,000 ft	1,001–2,000 ft	2,001–4,000 ft	4,001–6,000 ft	6,001–8,000 ft
Dial Gauge	Pint	55	11		12	13	14
	Quart	85	11		12	13	14
Weighted Gauge	Pint	55	10	15			
	Quart	85	10	15			

Nutrition Facts (per 100g serving):

Nutrient	Amount
Calories	1 kcal
Total Fat	0 g
Carbohydrates	0.3 g
Sodium	233 mg

PEAS

Canning peas is an excellent way to preserve their flavor and nutritional value for future use. This beginner-friendly recipe focuses on both the selection and the canning process to ensure the best quality canned peas.

Ingredients

- **Peas in pods**: 2 kg for a quart jar or 1 kg for a pint jar

- **Salt**: One teaspoon per quart jar (optional)

- **Water**

Selection of Peas

If you're using sugar snaps or Chinese edible pods, freezing them first is recommended. Always choose pods that are tender, young, and sweet, and avoid using any diseased pods.

Procedure

Step 1: Preparing the Peas

Hot Packing Method: Boil the peas in a saucepan for two minutes. Transfer the hot peas into preheated jars and add cooking liquid or boiling water. Optionally, add salt.

Raw Packing Method: Fill the preheated jars with raw peas and add boiling water. Do not press or shake the peas in the jar.

Important: Regardless of the packing method, ensure you leave one inch of headspace in the jar.

Step 2: Final Steps

- Debubble the jars to remove air pockets.

- Clean the rims of the jars to ensure a proper seal.

- Adjust the lid and place the jars in the canner.

Recommended Processing Times

Type of Canner	Jar Size	Process Time (in minutes)	Canner Pressure (in lb)				
			0–1,000 ft	1,001–2,000 ft	2,001–4,000 ft	4,001–6,000 ft	6,001–8,000 ft
Dial Gauge	Pint or Quart	40	11		12	13	14
Weighted Gauge	Pint or Quart	40	10	15			

Weighted Gauge Canner: For both pint or quart jars, process for 40 minutes. Pressure should be 10 lbs for altitudes up to 1,000 ft and 15 lbs for altitudes above 1,000 ft.

Nutrition Facts per Serving

Nutrient	Amount
Calories	81 kcal
Total Fat	0.4 g
Saturated Fat	0.1 g
Carbohydrates	14.5 g
Sugars	5.7 g
Sodium	121 mg
Cholesterol	0 mg
Protein	5.4 g
Calcium	25 mg
Potassium	244 mg

Nutrient	Amount
Iron	1 mg

SWEET POTATOES

Time: 1 hour 30 minutes

Serving Size: Varies (depends on the number of jars)**Prep Time**: 30 minutes

Processing Time: 1 hour

Description:

Sweet potatoes are nutritious, filling, and versatile. This pressure canning recipe will help you preserve them for later use. This guide uses the hot packing method and is intended for small to medium-sized sweet potatoes.

Skill Level: Intermediate

Special Equipment: Pressure canner, canning jars (pint or quart size)

Safety Considerations:

- Only use the hot packing method for sweet potatoes.

- Do not attempt to dry-pack.

Ingredients:

- Sweet potatoes (1 kg per quart jar or 1/2 kg per pint jar)

- Water or syrup for covering

- Salt (1 teaspoon per quart jar, optional)

Tools Needed:

- Pressure canner

- Canning jars (pint or quart size)

- Saucepan for boiling or steaming

- Peeler

- Measuring spoons

Directions:

1. **Preparation**: Wash the sweet potatoes. Boil or steam them for 15-20 minutes, or until they are partially soft.

2. **Peeling and Cutting**: After boiling, peel off the skin and cut the potatoes into uniform sizes. Do not mash them.

3. **Packing**: Place the prepared sweet potatoes into your preheated canning jars, ensuring you leave about an inch of headspace.

4. **Adding Liquids**: Pour boiling water or syrup over the sweet potatoes in the jars. Optionally, you can add salt.

5. **Finishing Steps**: Debubble the jars and check that the headspace is still one inch. Wipe the rims clean and adjust the lids before sealing.

To process your sweet potatoes, follow the processing time and pressure below:

Type of Canner	Jar Size	Process Time (in minutes)	Canner Pressure (in lb)				
			0–1,000 ft	1,001–2,000 ft	2,001–4,000 ft	4,001–6,000 ft	6,001–8,000 ft
Dial Gauge	Pint	65	11		12	13	14
	Quart	90	11		12	13	14
Weighted Gauge	Pint	65	10	15			
	Quart	90	10	15			

Nutrition Facts per 100g Serving

Nutrition Component	Amount
Calories	118 kcal
Total Fat	0.2 g
Saturated Fat	0 g
Carbohydrates	27.9 g
Total Sugars	0.5 g
Sodium	242 mg
Cholesterol	0 mg
Protein	1.5 g
Calcium	17 mg
Potassium	816 mg
Iron	1 mg

By following this recipe, you can enjoy the richness and versatility of sweet potatoes in your meals for months to come.

PRESSURE CANNING WHITE POTATOES

Time: 1 hour 45 minutes

Serving Size: Varies (depends on the number of jars)

Prep Time: 45 minutes

Processing Time: 1 hour

Description:

Preserve the goodness of white potatoes through pressure canning. This method allows you to have a stock of this staple food, perfect for emergency situations or quick meal prep. The following recipe ensures the quality and safety of your canned potatoes.

Skill Level: Advanced

Special Equipment: Pressure canner, ascorbic acid solution

Safety Considerations:

- Potatoes stored below 45°F may discolor when canned.

- Use ascorbic acid solution to prevent discoloration.

Ingredients:

- White potatoes (about 1.2 kg per quart or 600 grams per pint jar)

- Ascorbic acid solution

- Salt (1 teaspoon per quart or 1/2 teaspoon per pint)

- Water

Tools Needed:

- Pressure canner

- Canning jars (pint or quart size)

- Large bowl for ascorbic acid solution

- Measuring spoons

- Saucepan for boiling

Directions:

1. **Preparation**: Wash and peel the white potatoes. To prevent discoloration, soak them in an ascorbic acid solution. This can be made from 3 grams of ascorbic acid dissolved in one gallon of cold water.

2. **Cutting**: Either leave the potatoes whole or cut them into about half-inch cubes.

3. **Pre-Cooking**: Drain the ascorbic acid solution. For cubed potatoes, cook in boiling water for two minutes, then drain again. For whole potatoes, boil for ten minutes and drain.

4. **Seasoning**: Add 1 teaspoon of salt per quart or 1/2 teaspoon per pint.

5. **Packing**: Place the hot potatoes into preheated jars, leaving an inch of headspace. Add hot water to cover.

6. **Finishing Steps**: Debubble your jars. Wipe the rims clean and adjust the lids before sealing.

To process your white potatoes, follow these recommended processing times and pressures:

Type of Canner	Jar Size	Process Time (in minutes)	Canner Pressure (in lb)				
			0–1,000 ft	1,001–2,000 ft	2,001–4,000 ft	4,001–6,000 ft	6,001–8,000 ft
	Pint	35	11		12	13	14

Dial Gauge	Quart	40	11		12	13	14
Weighted Gauge	Pint	35	10	15			
	Quart	40	10	15			

Nutrition Facts per 100g Serving

Nutrition Component	Amount
Calories	77 kcal
Total Fat	0.1 g
Saturated Fat	0 g
Carbohydrates	17.5 g
Total Sugars	0.8 g
Sodium	200 mg
Cholesterol	0 mg
Protein	2 g
Calcium	12 mg
Potassium	421 mg
Iron	1 mg

By adhering to this pressure canning guide for white potatoes, you will be able to preserve their quality and extend their shelf life, making them a ready-to-use ingredient for various recipes.

SPINACH

Time: 1 hour 30 minutes

Serving Size: Varies (depends on the number of jars)

Prep Time: 30 minutes

Processing Time: 1 hour

Description:

Preserve the nutritional goodness of spinach and other greens by pressure canning them. This method is particularly useful for extending the shelf life of these nutrient-dense vegetables. Here's a step-by-step guide to help you safely and effectively can spinach or other greens.

Skill Level: Intermediate

Special Equipment: Pressure canner, cheesecloth bag

Safety Considerations:

- Use freshly harvested greens only.
- Do not can wilted, discolored, or insect-damaged greens.

Tools Needed:

- Pressure canner

- Canning jars (pint or quart size)

- Cheesecloth bag

- Large bowls for washing

- Measuring spoons

- Saucepan for boiling water

Directions:

1. Preparation: Wash the greens in batches and drain well. Repeat the process until the drained water is clear and free from grit.

2. Trimming: Cut away tough stems and remove the midribs from the leaves.

3. Steaming: Place the greens in a cheesecloth bag and steam for 3–5 minutes, or until they have wilted. If processing a large amount, steam about half a kilo at a time.

4. Packing: Place the hot, wilted greens into preheated jars and cover them with boiling water. Add salt to taste, if desired.

5. Finishing Steps: Debubble your jars, clean the rims, and adjust the lids before sealing.

To ensure that you process your greens safely, follow these recommended processing times and pressures:

Type of Canner	Jar Size	Process Time (in minutes)	Canner Pressure (in lb)				
			0–1,000 ft	1,001–2,000 ft	2,001–4,000 ft	4,001–6,000 ft	6,001–8,000 ft
Dial Gauge	Pint	70	11		12	13	14
	Quart	90	11		12	13	14
Weighted Gauge	Pint	70	10	15			
	Quart	90	10	15			

Nutrition Facts per 100g Serving

Nutrition Component	Amount
Calories	23 kcal
Total Fat	0.4 g
Saturated Fat	0.1 g

Nutrition Component	Amount
Carbohydrates	3.6 g
Total Sugars	0.4 g
Sodium	79 mg
Cholesterol	0 mg
Protein	2.9 g
Calcium	99 mg
Potassium	558 mg
Iron	2.7 mg

By following this recipe, you can keep a stockpile of nutrient-rich greens like spinach, ready to be used in various recipes whenever you need them.

PRESSURE CANNING BAKED BEANS

Time: 6-7 hours

Serving Size: Varies (depends on the number of jars)

Prep Time: 2 hours

Processing Time: 4-5 hours (baking time)

Description:

Learn how to make delicious baked beans that you can preserve for later use. This recipe guides you through the process of preparing the beans, creating a molasses sauce, and pressure canning the final product for long-term storage.

Skill Level: Intermediate

Special Equipment: Pressure canner, baking crock/casserole/pan

Safety Considerations:

- Ensure all canning jars and lids are properly sterilized.

Ingredients:

- Beans (340 g per quart or 170 g per pint)
- **For Molasses Sauce:**
    - Water or cooking liquid from beans (4 cups)
    - Vinegar (1 tablespoon)
    - Dark molasses (3 tablespoons)
    - Salt (2 tablespoons)
    - Powdered dry mustard (3/4 teaspoon)
- Water for soaking beans
- Pork, ham, or bacon

Tools Needed:

- Pressure canner
- Canning jars (pint or quart size)
- Baking crock, casserole, or pan

- Measuring cups and spoons
- Saucepan

Directions:

1. **Preparation**: Soak and boil the beans. Prepare the molasses sauce by mixing the ingredients and bringing it to a boil.
2. **Baking**: Place your choice of meat in a baking crock, casserole, or pan. Add the beans and cover them with the molasses sauce. Bake at 350°F for 4-5 hours, adding water every hour if needed.
3. **Canning**: After baking, transfer the beans to preheated canning jars, leaving one inch of headspace.
4. **Finishing Steps**: Debubble your jars, wipe off any excess food from the rims, and adjust the lids before sealing.

To process your beans, here are the processing times and pressures you should follow:

Type of Canner	Jar Size	Process Time (in minutes)	Canner Pressure (in lb)				
			0–1,000 ft	1,001–2,000 ft	2,001–4,000 ft	4,001–6,000 ft	6,001–8,000 ft
Dial Gauge	Pint	65	11		12	13	14
	Quart	75	11		12	13	14
Weighted Gauge	Pint	65	10	15			
	Quart	75	10	15			

Nutrition Facts per 100g Serving

Nutrition Component	Amount
Calories	240 kcal
Total Fat	0.9 g
Saturated Fat	0.3 g
Carbohydrates	53.9 g
Total Sugars	37.4 g

Nutrition Component	Amount
Sodium	970 mg
Cholesterol	15 mg
Protein	6.5 g
Calcium	161 mg
Potassium	1187 mg
Iron	4 mg

This recipe allows you to have delicious, home-cooked baked beans readily available. The convenience of canned baked beans combined with homemade taste is unbeatable.

BEANS WITH TOMATO OR MOLASSES SAUCE

Time: 3-4 hours

Serving Size: Varies

Prep Time: 2 hours

Processing Time: 1-2 hours

Description:

This recipe is a versatile method for canning beans with either a tomato-based sauce or molasses sauce. This is a non-baked version of canned beans.

Skill Level: Intermediate

Special Equipment: Pressure canner

Safety Considerations:

- Make sure to sterilize all canning jars and lids.

Ingredients:

- Dry beans (340 g per quart or 170 g per pint)

- **For Molasses Sauce**: See baked beans recipe

- **For Tomato Sauce**: Choose one of the following combinations

    - Tomato juice (1 qt), salt (2 tsp), sugar (3 tbsp), chopped onion (1 tbsp), allspice (1/4 tsp), ground cloves (1/4 tsp), mace (1/4 tsp), cayenne pepper (1/4 tsp)

    - Cooking liquid from beans (3 cups), tomato ketchup (1 cup)

- Pork, ham, or bacon

- Water for boiling beans

Nutrition Facts per 100g Serving

Same as baked beans recipe.

Directions:

1. Sort and wash the dry beans.

2. Add 3 cups of water per cup of dry beans and bring to a boil. Let soak for an hour, then drain.

3. Boil the beans in fresh water and drain again, saving the water for the sauce.

4. Prepare your choice of sauce by mixing the indicated ingredients and bringing it to a boil.

5. Fill preheated jars with 3/4 full of beans, add meat, and then the sauce, leaving a one-inch headspace.

6. Debubble jars, wipe rims, adjust lids and process.

PRESSURE CANNING FRESH LIMA BEANS

Time: 2-3 hours

Serving Size: Varies

Prep Time: 1 hour

Processing Time: 1-2 hours

Description:

This recipe provides you the flexibility to can fresh lima beans using either a hot or raw packing method.

Skill Level: Intermediate

Special Equipment: Pressure canner

Safety Considerations:

- Make sure to sterilize all canning jars and lids.

Ingredients:

- Fresh lima beans (about 1.7 kg per quart; about 850 g per pint jar)

- Salt (1 tsp per quart; 1/2 tsp per pint)

- Water

This recipe for lima beans requires different processing time and pressure compared to the baked beans and beans with tomato sauce or molasses sauce recipes. The table below shows the recommended data for the pressure-canned lima bean recipe:

Type of Canner	Jar Size		Canner Pressure (in lb)

		Process Time (in minutes)	0–1,000 ft	1,001–2,000 ft	2,001–4,000 ft	4,001–6,000 ft	6,001–8,000 ft
Dial Gauge	Pint	40	11		12	13	14
	Quart	50	11		12	13	14
Weighted Gauge	Pint	40	10	15			
	Quart	50	10	15			

Directions:
1. Remove seeds from pods and wash thoroughly.
2. Choose either hot or raw packing method:
   a. **Hot Pack**: Boil beans in water, then place in preheated jars with a one-inch headspace.
   b. **Raw Pack**: Place raw beans in preheated jars without pressing them down. Leave adequate headspace.
3. Add salt and fresh boiling water, respecting the one-inch headspace.
4. Debubble jars, wipe rims, adjust lids, and process.

Nutrition Facts per 100g Serving

Nutrition Component	**Amount**
Calories	120 kcal
Total Fat	0.9 g
Saturated Fat	0.2 g
Carbohydrates	21.4 g
Total Sugars	1.6 g
Sodium	156 mg
Cholesterol	0 mg
Protein	7.3 g
Calcium	36 mg

Nutrition Component	Amount
Potassium	496 mg
Iron	3 mg

PRESSURE CANNING SNAP AND ITALIAN BEANS

Time: 1-2 hours

Serving Size: Varies

Prep Time: 30 minutes

Processing Time: 30 minutes - 1 hour

Description:

This is a simple and quick recipe for canning snap and Italian beans. It offers both hot and raw packing methods to suit your needs.

Skill Level: Beginner

Special Equipment: Pressure canner

Safety Considerations:

- Make sure to sterilize all canning jars and lids before use.

Ingredients:

- Snap and Italian beans (about 850 grams per quart or about 425 grams per pint)

- Salt (1 teaspoon per quart or 1/2 teaspoon per pint jar)

- Boiling water

Directions:

1. Wash and trim the beans. You can either leave the pods whole or cut them into 1-inch pieces.

2. Choose your preferred packing method:
   a. **Hot Packing**: Place the beans in a pan and cover with boiling water. Boil for five minutes. Then, pack the hot beans into your preheated canning jars, leaving

a one-inch headspace.

b. **Raw Packing**: Place the raw beans in your preheated canning jars, also leaving a one-inch headspace.

3. Pour boiling water over the beans, maintaining the one-inch headspace. Add salt if desired.

4. Debubble your canning jars, wipe the rims with a damp paper towel, adjust the lids, and process.

This recipe requires less processing time compared to the other bean recipes. To ensure that you do not overprocess your snap or Italian beans, follow the table below:

Type of Canner	Jar Size	Process Time (in minutes)	Canner Pressure (in lb)				
			0–1,000 ft	1,001–2,000 ft	2,001–4,000 ft	4,001–6,000 ft	6,001–8,000 ft
Dial Gauge	Pint	20	11		12	13	14
	Quart	25	11		12	13	14
Weighted Gauge	Pint	20	10	15			
	Quart	25	10	15			

Nutrition Facts per 100g Serving

Nutrition Component	Amount
Calories	37 kcal
Total Fat	0.3 g
Saturated Fat	0.1 g
Carbohydrates	8.4 g
Total Sugars	1.7 g
Sodium	292 mg

Nutrition Component	Amount
Cholesterol	0 mg
Protein	2 g
Calcium	47 mg
Potassium	155 mg
Iron	1 mg

OKRA

Time: 1-2 hours

Serving Size: Varies

Prep Time: 30 minutes

Processing Time: 30 minutes - 1 hour

Description:

This recipe is ideal for those who enjoy okra and its nutritional benefits. It is a straightforward recipe that uses the hot packing method to prepare the okra for canning.

Skill Level: Beginner

Special Equipment: Pressure canner

Safety Considerations:

- Sterilize all canning jars and lids before use.

Ingredients:

- Okra (700 grams per quart or 350 grams per pint jar)

- Salt (1 teaspoon per quart or 1/2 teaspoon per pint jar)

- Boiling water

Directions:

1. **Preparation**: Wash the okra and trim the ends. You can either leave them whole or cut them into 1-inch pieces.

2. **Boiling**: Place the okra in a saucepan and cover with hot water. Boil for two minutes. Drain the water.

3. **Packing**: Place the hot okra in your preheated canning jars. Fill with boiling water or the cooking liquid from the boiled okra, leaving a one-inch headspace. Optionally, add salt.

4. **Final Steps**: Debubble your canning jars, wipe the rims with a damp paper towel, adjust the lids, and your jars are ready for processing.

To process your okra, be mindful of the processing time and pressure recommended, as shown in the table below:

Type of Canner	Jar Size	Process Time (in minutes)	Canner Pressure (in lb)				
			0–1,000 ft	1,001–2,000 ft	2,001–4,000 ft	4,001–6,000 ft	6,001–8,000 ft
Dial Gauge	Pint	25	11		12	13	14
	Quart	40	11		12	13	14
Weighted Gauge	Pint	25	10	15			
	Quart	40	10	15			

Nutrition Facts per 100g Serving

Nutrition Component	Amount
Calories	40 kcal
Total Fat	0.2 g
Saturated Fat	0 g
Carbohydrates	7.5 g
Total Sugars	1.5 g
Sodium	340 mg
Cholesterol	0 mg
Protein	1.9 g
Calcium	82 mg
Potassium	299 mg
Iron	1 mg

PUMPKINS OR WINTER SQUASH

Time: 1-2 hours

Serving Size: Varies

Prep Time: 30 minutes

Processing Time: 30 minutes - 1 hour

Description:

Enjoy the flavors of fall all year round with this pressure canning recipe for cubed pumpkins or winter squash. Remember to use only small, hard-rind, and stringless pumpkins or squash for the best results. This recipe uses the hot packing method.

Skill Level: Intermediate

Special Equipment: Pressure canner

Safety Considerations:

- Sterilize all canning jars and lids before use.

- Do not mash or puree the pumpkins or squash.

Ingredients:

- Pumpkin or winter squash (one kg per quart or 500 grams per pint jar)

- Boiling water

Directions:

1. **Preparation**: Wash the pumpkins or winter squash. Peel them and discard the seeds. Cut into 1-inch pieces.

2. **Boiling**: Place the pumpkin or squash pieces into a saucepan and cover with water. Boil for two minutes, being careful not to mash or puree them.

3. **Packing**: Fill your preheated canning jars with hot pumpkins or squash, and top with cooking liquid. Leave a one-inch headspace.

4. **Final Steps**: Debubble your canning jars, wipe the rims with a damp paper towel, adjust the lids, and your jars are ready for processing.

To process your canned pumpkins in a pressure canner, be wary of the recommended processing time and pressure as indicated in the table below:

Type of Canner	Jar Size	Process Time (in minutes)	Canner Pressure (in lb)				
			0–1,000 ft	1,001–2,000 ft	2,001–4,000 ft	4,001–6,000 ft	6,001–8,000 ft
Dial Gauge	Pint	55	11		12	13	14
	Quart	90	11		12	13	14
Weighted Gauge	Pint	55	10	15			
	Quart	90	10	15			

Nutrition Facts per 100g Serving

Nutrition Component	Amount
Calories	34 kcal
Total Fat	0.3 g
Saturated Fat	0.2 g
Carbohydrates	8.1 g
Total Sugars	3.3 g
Sodium	703 mg
Cholesterol	0 mg
Protein	1.1 g
Calcium	26 mg
Potassium	206 mg
Iron	1 mg

This recipe allows you to enjoy pumpkins or winter squash in a convenient, preserved form. Whether you're whipping up a quick soup or adding some to a stew, these canned cubes will make your life easier. Happy canning!

MIXED VEGETABLES

Time: 1.5-2 hours

Serving Size: 7 quarts

Prep Time: 45 minutes

Processing Time: 45 minutes - 1 hour

Description:

Pressure-canning mixed vegetables allows you to enjoy a variety of veggies year-round. This recipe is easy to follow and versatile, giving you the freedom to substitute or adjust vegetable quantities to your liking. Great for beginners and a convenient meal solution for busy families.

Skill Level: Beginner

Special Equipment: Pressure canner

Safety Considerations:

- Sterilize all canning jars and lids before use.

- Avoid adding dried beans, cream-style corn, leafy greens, sweet potatoes, or squash.

Ingredients:

- Zucchini (4 cups)

- Carrots (6 cups)

- Lima Beans (6 cups)

- Green Beans (6 cups)

- Tomatoes (4 cups)

- Sweet Corn (6 cups)

- Salt (1 teaspoon per quart jar)

- Boiling water

Directions:

1. **Preparation:** Prepare each vegetable as you normally would. For zucchini, wash, trim, and cube it. For tomatoes, blanch them for 30-60 seconds, cool in cold water, and remove skins and cores.

2. **Cooking:** Combine all prepared vegetables in a large pot. Cover with water and add salt (1 teaspoon per quart). Bring the mixture to a boil for 5 minutes.

3. **Packing:** Fill your preheated jars with the hot vegetable mixture and cooking liquid, leaving a one-inch headspace.

4. **Final Steps:** Debubble the jars and wipe the rims clean. Adjust the lids and prepare for processing.

To process your mixed vegetables, follow the table below for the recommended processing time and pressure:

Type of Canner	Jar Size	Process Time (in minutes)	Canner Pressure (in lb)				
			0–1,000 ft	1,001–2,000 ft	2,001–4,000 ft	4,001–6,000 ft	6,001–8,000 ft
Dial Gauge	Pint	75	11		12	13	14
	Quart	90	11		12	13	14
Weighted Gauge	Pint	75	10	15			
	Quart	90	10	15			

Nutrition Facts per Quart

Nutrition Component	Amount
Calories	184 kcal
Total Fat	1.5 g
Saturated Fat	0.3 g
Carbohydrates	34.2 g
Total Sugars	4.2 g
Sodium	48 mg
Cholesterol	0 mg
Protein	10.6 g
Calcium	58 mg
Potassium	843 mg
Iron	5 mg

Chapter 8:

RECIPES FOR PRESSURE CANNING SOUPS AND STEWS

Soups and stews can be a great addition to your pantry. These kinds of foods can just be heated, and your family can instantly enjoy a hearty and hot meal. We all know that soups and stews are really perfect for cold days. These kinds of foods are also easy to eat for children. Whenever a family member falls ill, serving them soup can help them satisfy their hunger easily. There are various soup and stew recipes that you can pressure cook. List down the ingredients you need and get ready to prepare and process them. Follow the recipes written in this chapter to ensure food quality and safety.

CHICKEN SOUP

An easy meal to serve your family when any member is under the weather is chicken soup. Hence, this is a great addition to your pantry, as you already have stock in hand and won't need to cook chicken soup from scratch. After all, when a family member is sick, you should focus your time on taking care of them instead of spending it preparing their meals from scratch. This recipe I will share with you is easy to process and will just need reheating before consumption. You can even turn it into chicken noodle soup by just adding noodles after the soup has been reheated. You may also just serve it with rice. Or you may serve it with chicken dumplings, if available. This recipe is really versatile and, thus, worth processing.

Time: 2-3 hours

Serving Size: Varies (Calculated per quart)

Prep Time: 1 hour

Processing Time: 1-2 hours

Description:

A pantry staple, this canned chicken soup offers the comfort of homemade soup without the hassle. Easy to prepare and heat-pack, this versatile soup can be turned into chicken noodle soup, served with rice, or paired with dumplings. The perfect remedy when someone in the family is feeling under the weather.

Skill Level: Intermediate

Special Equipment: Pressure canner

Safety Considerations:

- Sterilize all canning jars and lids before use.

- Avoid adding rice, flour, pasta, cream, milk, or other thickeners.

Ingredients:

- Chicken (diced and cooked, 350 g per quart jar)

- Chicken Stock (1 cup per quart jar)

- Celery (chopped, 3/4 cup per quart jar)

- Carrots (sliced, 3/4 cup per quart jar)

- Onion (chopped, 1/4 cup per quart jar)

- Salt (optional)

- Pepper (optional)

Directions:

1. **Preparation**: Wash, peel, and chop carrots; dice celery and onion. Cook chicken until tender, either shredded or cubed.

2. **Cooking**: In a large pot, combine chicken, vegetables, and chicken stock. Bring to a boil and simmer for 5-10 minutes. Season with salt and pepper, if desired.

3. **Packing**: Fill preheated jars halfway with solids. Top with broth, leaving one-inch headspace.

4. **Final Steps**: Debubble jars and wipe rims. Adjust lids and prepare for processing.

To ensure that you safely process your chicken soup, follow the recommended processing time and pressure shown in the table below:

Type of Canner	Jar Size	Process Time (in minutes)	Canner Pressure (in lb)				
			0–1,000 ft	1,001–2,000 ft	2,001–4,000 ft	4,001–6,000 ft	6,001–8,000 ft
Dial Gauge	Pint	60	11		12	13	14
	Quart	75	11		12	13	14
Weighted Gauge	Pint	60	10	15			
	Quart	75	10	15			

Nutrition Facts per Quart

Nutrition Component	Amount
Calories	606 kcal
Total Fat	11.3 g
Saturated Fat	3.2 g
Carbohydrates	16.2 g
Total Sugars	8.2 g
Sodium	3438 mg
Cholesterol	270 mg
Protein	103.9 g

Nutrition Component	Amount
Calcium	133 mg
Potassium	1233 mg
Iron	4 mg

PRESSURE-CANNED CHICKEN STOCK

Time: ~2 hours (excluding overnight freezing)

Serving Size: Varies (Calculated per 100g serving)

Prep Time: 1 hour

Processing Time: 1 hour 25 minutes

Description:

Chicken stock is a versatile kitchen staple that enhances many recipes. Learn to make your own pressure-canned chicken stock, and you'll have a convenient, healthier alternative to store-bought versions. Ideal for various recipes, including the canned chicken soup mentioned earlier.

Skill Level: Intermediate

Special Equipment: Pressure canner

Safety Considerations:

- Sterilize all canning jars and lids before use.

- Do not add any fats, cream, or thickeners.

Ingredients:

- Chicken bones or carcass

- Water

- Bay leaf (optional)

Directions:

1. **Preparation**: Remove all meat from the chicken bones or carcass. The meat can be used in other recipes.

2. **Optional Step**: For a richer flavor, roast the bones for about an hour.

3. **Boiling**: In a large pot, cover bones with water, bring to a boil, then simmer for 45 minutes. Add bay leaf for additional flavor if desired.

4. **Straining**: Remove bones and any leftover meat from the stock.

5. **Freezing**: Freeze the stock overnight.

6. **Defatting**: Scrape off and discard the fat layer from the top of the frozen stock.

7. **Packing**: Reheat the stock and fill your preheated jars, leaving an inch of headspace. Debubble jars, wipe rims, and adjust lids for processing.

Adjust the lids and follow the table below for the processing time and pressure.

Type of Canner	Jar Size	Process Time (in minutes)	Canner Pressure (in lb)				
			0–1,000 ft	1,001–2,000 ft	2,001–4,000 ft	4,001–6,000 ft	6,001–8,000 ft
Dial Gauge	Pint	20	11		12	13	14
	Quart	25	11		12	13	14
Weighted Gauge	Pint	20	10	15			
	Quart	25	10	15			

Nutrition Facts per 100g Serving

Nutrition Component	Amount
Calories	7 kcal
Total Fat	0 g
Saturated Fat	0 g
Carbohydrates	0.7 g

Nutrition Component	Amount
Total Sugars	0.7 g
Sodium	27 mg
Cholesterol	0 mg
Protein	0.7 g
Calcium	0 mg
Potassium	67 mg
Iron	0 mg

Once you've prepared and processed this chicken stock, it's ready to be added to your pantry for future recipes. Enjoy your cooking adventures with the added convenience of homemade chicken stock!

BEEF STEW

Time: Varies

Serving Size: 1 quart (Nutrition calculated per quart)

Prep Time: Varies

Processing Time: Varies

Description:

Enjoy a hearty, homemade beef stew without the fuss. Ideal for a quick, nutritious family meal, this pressure-canned beef stew just needs reheating.

Skill Level: Intermediate

Special Equipment: Pressure canner

Safety Considerations:

- Sterilize all canning jars and lids before use.

- Always debubble your canning jars and clean the rims for proper sealing.

Ingredients:

- Chuck roast (250 g per quart jar)

- Onion (1/3 of a piece per quart)

- Celery (one stalk per quart)

- Carrot (1/4 of a piece per quart)

- Potato (one piece per quart)

- Salt (1 tablespoon per quart, optional)

- Bouillon (2/3 tablespoon per quart)

- Water

Directions:

1. **Prepare Bouillon**: In a pot, combine 2/3 cup of bouillon with 2 cups of water. Bring to a boil.

2. **Preparation**: Wash, peel, and chop potatoes, onions, carrots, and celery.

3. **Meat Preparation**: Ensure your beef is already roasted or stewed.

4. **Packing**: In your preheated jars, layer beef, onions, celery, carrots, and potatoes. Pour hot bouillon over the ingredients, leaving an inch of headspace. Add salt if desired.

5. **Final Steps**: Debubble your jars, wipe rims, and adjust lids for processing.

To make sure that you process your beef stew safely and successfully, follow these recommended processing times and pressures:

Type of Canner	Jar Size	Process Time (in minutes)	Canner Pressure (in lb)				
			0–1,000 ft	1,001–2,000 ft	2,001–4,000 ft	4,001–6,000 ft	6,001–8,000 ft
Dial Gauge	Pint	75	11		12	13	14
	Quart	90	11		12	13	14
Weighted Gauge	Pint	75	10	15			
	Quart	90	10	15			

Nutrition Facts per Quart

Nutrition Component	Amount
Calories	641 kcal
Total Fat	29 g
Saturated Fat	10 g

Nutrition Component	Amount
Carbohydrates	40.2 g
Total Sugars	5.1 g
Sodium	8105 mg
Cholesterol	166 mg
Protein	50.7 g
Calcium	45 mg
Potassium	1024 mg
Iron	7 mg

BEEF STOCK

Beef stock, like chicken stock, can be a great addition to your pantry. You can easily use it in various recipes. It is better to have homemade canned beef stock than to buy commercial broths or stocks from stores. With home canning, you can control the ingredients you add to your broth. You can make sure that you only use safe and high-quality ingredients. Preparing and processing beef stock is similar to that of chicken stock.

Time: 4 hours

Serving Size: 1 cup (Nutrition calculated per cup)

Prep Time: 10 minutes

Processing Time: Varies

Description:

Homemade canned beef stock offers greater control over your ingredients, yielding a healthier, richer base for countless recipes. Perfect for soups, stews, and gravies.

Skill Level: Intermediate

Special Equipment: Pressure canner, stockpot

Safety Considerations:

- Sterilize all canning jars and lids before use.

- Always debubble your canning jars and clean the rims for proper sealing.

Ingredients:

- Beef bones (sawed or cracked, freshly trimmed)

- Water

Directions:

1. **Initial Boil**: Rinse beef bones and place them in a stockpot. Cover the bones completely with water.

2. **Cook**: Bring the water to a boil, then reduce to a simmer and cook for 3-4 hours.

3. **Remove Bones and Fat**: Remove bones from the stock and let it cool. Skim off any excess fat.

4. **Optional**: Remove any remaining meat tidbits from the bones and re-extract flavors by simmering them in the same stock again.

5. **Final Steps**: Once the stock is cool, reheat it and pour into your sterilized canning jars, leaving an inch of headspace. Debubble the jars, wipe the rims clean, and adjust the lids. Ready for pressure canning.

Follow the table below for the recommended processing time and pressure.

Type of Canner	Jar Size	Process Time (in minutes)	Canner Pressure (in lb)				
			0–1,000 ft	1,001–2,000 ft	2,001–4,000 ft	4,001–6,000 ft	6,001–8,000 ft
Dial Gauge	Pint	75	11		12	13	14
	Quart	90	11		12	13	14
Weighted Gauge	Pint	75	10	15			
	Quart	90	10	15			

Nutrition Facts per Cup

Nutrition Component	Amount
Calories	32 kcal
Total Fat	2.9 g
Saturated Fat	0.6 g
Carbohydrates	0 g
Total Sugars	0 g
Sodium	33.7 mg

Nutrition Component	Amount
Cholesterol	8.6 mg
Protein	1.7 g
Calcium	0 mg
Potassium	0 mg
Iron	0 mg

This beef stock is a pantry staple that you'll find yourself using often. It's a simple, wholesome addition to a range of dishes and it's easy to make and store. Happy canning!

Vegetable Soup

Time: 1 hour 15 minutes

Serving Size: 1 quart (Nutrition calculated per quart)

Prep Time: 20 minutes

Processing Time: Varies

Description:

Make the most of your garden produce or bulk vegetable shopping with this versatile vegetable soup recipe. Packed with nutritious vegetables, this pressure-canned soup makes for a convenient and healthy meal.

Skill Level: Intermediate

Special Equipment: Pressure canner, large pot

Safety Considerations:

- Always adhere to individual canning guidelines for each vegetable.

- No pasta, noodles, rice, or thickening agents should be added for safe canning.

Ingredients:

- Tomatoes (8 cups)

- White Potatoes (6 cups)

- Carrots (8 cups)

- Corn Whole Kernels (4 cups)

- Lima Beans (4 cups)

- Onions (2 cups)

- Salt (optional—1 teaspoon per quart)

- Pepper (optional)

- Water (6 cups, approx.)

Directions:

1. **Prepare Vegetables**: Refer to individual canning guidelines for each type of vegetable. Wash and prepare accordingly.

2. **Cooking**: In a large pot, combine all vegetables. Cover with approximately 6 cups of water. Over medium heat, bring the mixture to a boil and let it cook for about 15 minutes. Optionally, add salt and pepper to taste.

3. **Canning**: Pour the hot mixture into your sterilized and preheated canning jars. Make sure to leave an inch of headspace. Fill jars halfway with solids; the rest must be liquid.

4. **Final Steps**: Debubble your canning jars and wipe the rims with a damp paper towel. Adjust lids. The jars are now ready for pressure canning.

Follow the table below for the recommended processing times and pressure according to your pressure canner, jars, and altitude.

Type of Canner	Jar Size	Process Time (in minutes)	Canner Pressure (in lb)				
			0–1,000 ft	1,001–2,000 ft	2,001–4,000 ft	4,001–6,000 ft	6,001–8,000 ft
Dial Gauge	Pint	60	11		12	13	14
	Quart	75	11		12	13	14
Weighted Gauge	Pint	60	10	15			
	Quart	75	10	15			

Nutrition Facts per Quart

Nutrition Component	Amount
Calories	336 kcal

Nutrition Component	Amount
Total Fat	2.3 g
Saturated Fat	0.4 g
Carbohydrates	71.5 g
Total Sugars	19.4 g
Sodium	2468 mg
Cholesterol	0 mg
Protein	13.5 g
Calcium	124 mg
Potassium	1940 mg
Iron	5 mg

Feel free to adjust the proportions of the vegetables to suit your preferences. Enjoy your homemade canned vegetable soup, a handy and nutritious choice for quick meals!

PRESSURE-CANNED LENTIL SOUP

Time: 1 hour

Serving Size: 1 pint (Nutrition calculated per pint)

Prep Time: 20 minutes

Processing Time: Varies

Description:

Diversify your canned pantry with this nutritious and delicious lentil soup. Perfect for quick meals and a great way to introduce legumes to your family. This raw pack recipe doesn't require precooking, making it a beginner-friendly choice.

Skill Level: Beginner

Special Equipment: Pressure canner

Safety Considerations:

- Always adhere to canning guidelines for each ingredient.

- Make sure jars are only half filled with solids; the rest should be liquid.

Ingredients:

- Lentils (dry brown—1/2 cup per quart)

- Onions (4 tablespoons per quart)

- Tomatoes (1/2 cup per quart)

- Zucchini (1/2 cup per quart)

- Carrots (6 tablespoons per quart)

- Jalapeños (1 piece per quart)

- Kale (2/3 cup per quart)

- Salt (1 teaspoon per quart)

- Water or Chicken Broth (enough to cover)

Directions:

1. **Preparation:** Prepare each ingredient according to individual canning guidelines.

2. **Packing:** Using the raw packing method, add your ingredients to sterilized canning jars. Cover with water or chicken stock. Add salt to taste, if desired. Remember to only fill jars halfway with solids; the rest should be liquid.

3. **Final Steps:** Leave an inch of headspace, then debubble your jars. Wipe the rims to ensure a proper seal. Adjust the lids and process in a pressure canner according to guidelines.

Follow the recommended processing time and pressure for your canned lentil soup.

Type of Canner	Jar Size	Process Time (in minutes)	Canner Pressure (in lb)				
			0–1,000 ft	1,001–2,000 ft	2,001–4,000 ft	4,001–6,000 ft	6,001–8,000 ft
Dial Gauge	Pint	75	11		12	13	14
	Quart	90	11		12	13	14
Weighted Gauge	Pint	75	10	15			
	Quart	90	10	15			

Nutrition Facts per Pint

Nutrition Component	Amount
Calories	81 kcal
Total Fat	0.5 g

Nutrition Component	Amount
Saturated Fat	0.1 g
Carbohydrates	16 g
Total Sugars	3.8 g
Sodium	1190 mg
Cholesterol	0 mg
Protein	4.6 g
Calcium	56 mg
Potassium	466 mg
Iron	2 mg

Feel free to adjust the ingredients' proportions as per your family's preference. This lentil soup recipe not only adds variety to your pantry but also provides a quick, healthy meal option. Enjoy!

CHILI

Time: Varies (overnight soaking for dried beans)

Serving Size: 1 pint (Nutrition calculated per pint)

Yield: 9 pint jars

Prep Time: 1 hour

Processing Time: Varies

Description:

A hearty Tex-Mex favorite that will spice up mealtime! This pressure-canned chili recipe is a bit more complex, but the results are so satisfying you'll want to keep a couple of jars in your pantry at all times.

Skill Level: Intermediate

Special Equipment: Pressure canner, mesh strainer

Safety Considerations:

- Follow all safety precautions for pressure canning.

- Make sure to debubble your jars and clean the rims for a proper seal.

Ingredients:

- Kidney beans (500 g)

- Ground beef (1.5 kg)

- Onion (200 g)

- Crushed tomatoes (2 L)

- Pepper (150 g)

- Chili powder (1 tbsp)

- Ground black pepper (1 tbsp)

- Cumin (1 tbsp)

- Oregano (1 tbsp)

- Salt (2 tbsp)

- Garlic powder (1 tbsp)

Directions:

1. **Preparation**: If using dried beans, wash them and soak in water overnight. Drain.

2. **Boil Beans**: Place drained beans in a saucepan, cover with water, bring to a boil, and simmer for 30 minutes.

3. **Prepare Meat Mixture**: Chop onion and pepper. Mix with ground beef and brown in a saucepan. Drain excess grease using a mesh strainer.

4. **Combine**: In a large pot, combine drained beans, beef mixture, crushed tomatoes, and all seasonings. Bring to a boil, reduce heat, and simmer for 5 minutes.

5. **Pack Jars**: Fill preheated canning jars with hot chili, leaving one inch of headspace.

6. **Final Steps**: Debubble your jars and wipe the rims with a damp paper towel. Seal and process in a pressure canner according to guidelines.

The table below shows the recommended processing times and pressures to be followed:

Type of Canner	Jar Size	Process Time (in minutes)	Canner Pressure (in lb)				
			0–1,000 ft	1,001–2,000 ft	2,001–4,000 ft	4,001–6,000 ft	6,001–8,000 ft
Dial Gauge	Pint	75	11		12	13	14
Weighted Gauge	Pint	75	10	15			

Nutrition Facts per Pint

Nutrition Component	Amount
Calories	576 kcal
Total Fat	14.3 g
Saturated Fat	4.6 g
Carbohydrates	48.9 g
Total Sugars	4.2 g
Sodium	1712 mg
Cholesterol	149 mg
Protein	66.1 g
Calcium	104 mg
Potassium	1906 mg
Iron	38 mg

Feel free to adjust seasonings and remember to follow dietary restrictions. Keep this hearty chili on hand for a warm, comforting meal anytime!

BASIC CHILI FOR VARIETY

Time: Varies (overnight soaking for dried beans)

Serving Size: 1 pint (Nutrition calculated per pint)

Yield: 9 pint jars

Prep Time: 1 hour

Processing Time: Varies

Description:

Add variety to your pantry with this basic chili recipe. It offers a simpler seasoning profile compared to our previous chili recipe, perfect for those who appreciate straightforward flavors. You can switch between the two recipes to combat the law of diminishing marginal utility!

Skill Level: Intermediate

Special Equipment: Pressure canner, mesh strainer

Safety Considerations:

- Follow all safety guidelines for pressure canning.

- Properly debubble jars and clean the rims to ensure a secure seal.

Ingredients:

- Pinto beans (or red kidney beans), dried (3 cups)

- Ground beef (1.4 kg)

- Crushed tomatoes (2 L)

- Onions (1 1/2 cups)

- Peppers (1 cup)

- Salt (5 tsp)

- Chili powder (4 tbsp)

- Black pepper (1 tbsp)

- Water

Directions:

1. **Preparation:** Wash the dried beans, cover with water, and soak overnight. Drain and discard the water.

2. **Cook Beans:** Place soaked beans in a saucepan with 5.5 cups fresh water and 2 tsp salt. Bring to a boil, then simmer for 30 minutes. Drain and discard water.

3. **Brown Meat:** In another pan, brown ground beef, peppers, and onions. Use a mesh strainer to remove excess fat.

4. **Combine Ingredients:** Mix the cooked beans, beef mixture, crushed tomatoes, and remaining seasonings in a large pot. Simmer for 5 minutes.

5. **Pack Jars:** Fill preheated canning jars with the chili mixture, leaving 1-inch headspace. Debubble jars and wipe rims clean.

Type of Canner	Jar Size	Process Time (in minutes)	Canner Pressure (in lb)				
			0–1,000 ft	1,001–2,000 ft	2,001–4,000 ft	4,001–6,000 ft	6,001–8,000 ft
Dial Gauge	Pint	75	11		12	13	14
Weighted Gauge	Pint	75	10	15			

Nutrition Facts per Pint

Nutrition Component	Amount
Calories	555 kcal
Total Fat	12.7 g

Nutrition Component	Amount
Saturated Fat	4.2 g
Carbohydrates	48.9 g
Total Sugars	3.6 g
Sodium	1467 mg
Cholesterol	139 mg
Protein	63.3 g
Calcium	90 mg
Potassium	1821 mg
Iron	35 mg

Adjust seasoning according to taste and keep an eye on dietary restrictions. This basic chili recipe is a great addition to your pantry, offering a different flavor profile that's perfect for colder nights!

Chapter 9:

RECIPES FOR PRESSURE CANNING SEAFOOD

I love eating seafood. However, in some areas, seafood tends to be expensive. Aside from that, seafood also goes bad quickly. It will take up a lot of space in your freezer, especially if you are freezing seafood with shells. Growing up, seafood was my comfort food. I have a lot of seafood recipes that I am so excited to share with you. Although pressure canning seafood can be a little trickier than other meat products, I swear you and your family will enjoy eating these recipes. Well, unless you or a family member has a seafood allergy. Again, I would like to remind you to be careful with canning seafood, as the recipes and guidelines are more complicated. If you want to learn how to can seafood, then here are some guidelines and recipes I would like to share with you.

CLAMS

Clams are fun to eat. You can even add it to a lot of recipes, such as vongole pasta. However, this seafood will require careful handling and preparation to ensure food safety. I have adopted my clam recipe from the Institute of Food and Agricultural Sciences at the University of Florida. Thus, this recipe is safe to can. The preparation for this recipe is done by hot packing. You can make this recipe using pint or half-pint jars.

Time: Varies (depends on the number of clams)

Serving Size: 1 pint (Nutrition calculated per pint)

Yield: Varies (based on the number of clams)

Prep Time: 1 hour

Processing Time: Varies based on guidelines

Description:

A recipe that safely cans clams for a diverse pantry. Ideal for seafood lovers and perfect for dishes like vongole pasta. This recipe, adapted from the Institute of Food and Agricultural Sciences at the University of Florida, ensures food safety and quality.

Skill Level: Advanced

Special Equipment: Pressure canner, saucepan

Safety Considerations:

- Always prioritize safety when canning seafood.

- Follow all guidelines rigorously to ensure safe consumption.

- Use live clams and keep them alive on ice if there's a delay in processing.

Ingredients:

- Clams, live

- Water

- Salt (1/2 teaspoon per pint)

- Lemon juice or citric acid

Directions:

1. **Prompt Processing**: If you can't process immediately upon obtaining clams, ensure they remain alive and on ice.

2. **Clean Shells**: Scrub clam shells thoroughly to eliminate any dirt or sand. Rinse well.

3. **Steaming**: Steam the clams for 5 minutes. Open the shells and collect the clam meat. Retain the clam juice.

4. **Cleaning Clam Meat**: Prepare a mixture of water and 1 teaspoon of salt per quart. Use this to wash the clam meat. Rinse with fresh water afterward.

5. **Boiling**: Place clam meat in a saucepan and cover with boiling water mixed with either two tablespoons of lemon juice per gallon or 1/2 teaspoon of citric acid per gallon. Boil for 2 minutes and drain.

6. **Processing**: Optionally, mince or grind the clams using a food processor or meat grinder.

7. **Jar Filling**: Load preheated canning jars with clam meat. Pour over with hot clam juice. If short on clam juice, use hot water. Ensure 1-inch headspace.

8. **Sealing and Processing**: Debubble jars, wipe rims clean, and adjust lids. Follow the recommended processing time and pressure guidelines for safe preservation.

The recommended processing time and pressure for clams are shown in the table below. As seen in the table, clams are processed in half-pint or pint jars. Be sure to follow accordingly.

Type of Canner	Jar Size	Process Time (in minutes)	Canner Pressure (in lb)				
			0–1,000 ft	1,001–2,000 ft	2,001–4,000 ft	4,001–6,000 ft	6,001–8,000 ft
Dial Gauge	Half-Pint	60	11	11	12	13	14
	Pint	70	11	11	12	13	14
Weighted Gauge	Half-Pint	60	10	15	15	15	15
	Pint	70	10	15	15	15	15

Nutrition Facts per Pint

Nutrition Component	Amount
Calories	108 kcal
Total Fat	1.6 g
Saturated Fat	0.4 g
Carbohydrates	4.1 g
Total Sugars	0.6 g
Sodium	2408 mg

Nutrition Component	Amount
Cholesterol	46 mg
Protein	17.6 g
Calcium	66 mg
Potassium	465 mg
Iron	19 mg

This method ensures that the clams are safely preserved and ready for various dishes. Whether it's a simple seafood dish or an elaborate pasta recipe, these canned clams will come in handy!

SHRIMP

I can probably say that my family's favorite seafood is shrimp. Every member really enjoys eating shrimp from time to time. Shrimp, like other seafood, is canned in half-pint and pint jars. You should add canned shrimp to your pantry. Aside from being a delicious main course, it is also a low-calorie meal with a high protein content. Although the guidelines and recipe are more complicated, you will surely not regret learning this recipe. Just be careful if any of your family members are allergic to shrimp.

Time: Varies (depends on the number of shrimp)

Serving Size: 1 pint (Nutrition calculated per pint)

Yield: Varies (based on the number of shrimp)

Prep Time: 1 hour

Processing Time: Varies based on guidelines

Description:

Shrimp lovers, this is for you! Add a nutritious, low-calorie, and high-protein option to your pantry. Though the process may be intricate, the delicious outcome is worth it. A perfect main course or ingredient for various dishes.

Skill Level: Intermediate

Special Equipment: Canner, saucepan

Safety Considerations:

- Ensure that no family members are allergic to shrimp.

- Adhere strictly to the guidelines for food safety.

Ingredients:

- Shrimp

- Salt

- Vinegar

- Water

Directions:

1. **Freezing**: After removing the heads, freeze your shrimp. Only thaw when you're ready to can.

2. **Preparation**: For frozen shrimp, thaw first. Then rinse thoroughly with water and drain.

3. **Initial Boiling**: In a pot, combine water, 1/2 cup salt per gallon of water, and 1 cup vinegar per gallon. Add shrimp and boil for 8-10 minutes. Afterward, drain, rinse with cold water, and let cool.

4. **Salt Mixture (Optional)**: In a separate pot, mix water and 2 tablespoons of salt per gallon. Ensure salt dissolves before boiling. If preferred, you can skip this and use just hot water later.

5. **Peeling**: Once cooled, peel the shrimp.

6. **Jar Filling**: Pack preheated canning jars with the peeled shrimp. Ensure a 1-inch headspace. Pour the hot salt mixture or just hot water over the shrimp.

7. **Sealing and Processing**: Debubble jars, wipe rims to ensure a clean seal, and adjust lids. Follow the recommended processing time and pressure guidelines for safe preservation.

To ensure that the canned shrimp that you will stock in your pantry for future consumption remains safe, follow the table below for the recommended processing time and pressure. Again, start your timer once you have reached the recommended pressure.

Type of Canner	Jar Size	Process Time (in minutes)	Canner Pressure (in lb)				
			0–1,000 ft	1,001–2,000 ft	2,001–4,000 ft	4,001–6,000 ft	6,001–8,000 ft
Dial Gauge	Half-Pint or Pint	45	11		12	13	14
Weighted Gauge	Half-Pint or Pint	45	10	15			

Nutrition Facts per Pint

I have told you that shrimp are low in calories yet high in protein content. To support that, here is a table showing the nutrition facts for a pint jar of this canned shrimp recipe. Refer to this table to ensure that you serve your family the appropriate portion of this recipe.

Nutrition Component	Amount
Calories	298 kcal
Total Fat	4.2 g
Saturated Fat	1.3 g
Carbohydrates	3.9 g
Total Sugars	0 g
Sodium	1773 mg
Cholesterol	526 mg
Protein	56.9 g
Calcium	228 mg

Nutrition Component	Amount
Potassium	427 mg
Iron	1 mg

OYSTER

You may see oysters as expensive seafood. Thus, it would be beneficial if you learned how to preserve them. You can bulk buy oysters when they are cheap and process them for future consumption. The preparation and processing guidelines for oysters are similar to those for clams and shrimp. You need to prepare them using brine or a salt and water mixture. Processing oysters is a great skill to learn. Just be sure that you will serve this recipe to people who are not allergic to shellfish.

Time: Varies (depends on the number of oysters)

Serving Size: 1 pint (Nutrition calculated per pint)

Yield: Varies (based on the number of oysters)

Prep Time: 45 minutes

Processing Time: Varies based on guidelines

The two previous recipes for seafood that you learned required four ingredients, whereas this recipe is much simpler as it only requires three ingredients. Yet, this does not mean that pressure canning oysters are not as tedious as canning shrimp and clams. You still need to be careful with the preparation of your oysters to ensure food safety. In addition, just like clams and shrimp, oysters are processed in half-pint or pint jars. They must be kept on ice until they are to be canned.

Description:

Oysters, a delicacy for many, can be enjoyed year-round with this canning method. Preserve these marine gems for moments when you crave that distinctive oyster flavor, either on their own or in a dish.

Skill Level: Intermediate

Special Equipment: Canner, oven

Safety Considerations:

- Ensure none of the consumers are allergic to shellfish.

- Always maintain food safety standards throughout the process.

Ingredients:

- Oysters

- Water

- Salt

Directions:

1. **Preparation:** Thoroughly wash the oyster shells to eliminate any dirt or sand.

2. **Oven Heating:** Preheat the oven to 400° F. Place the oysters in the oven for 5-7 minutes. After heating, cool them momentarily in ice water.

3. **Shelling and Collection:** Drain and open the shells. Carefully extract and gather the oyster meat.

4. **Brining:** Mix water and 1/2 cup of salt per gallon. Utilize this brine to wash the oyster meat, and subsequently, drain them.

5. **Jar Filling:** Optionally, you can add 1/2 teaspoon of salt per pint jar. Place the drained oysters in your preheated canning jars. Cover them with boiling water, maintaining an inch of headspace.

6. **Sealing and Processing:** Debubble the jars, clean the rims with a dampened paper towel, adjust the lids, and proceed with the recommended processing time and pressure for safety.

Properly processed oysters will allow you to quickly serve your family various oyster dishes, even after several months of processing. To ensure that your oysters remain consumable after several months, follow the recommended processing time and pressure shown in the table below:

Type of Canner	Jar Size	Process Time (in minutes)	Canner Pressure (in lb)				
			0–1,000 ft	1,001–2,000 ft	2,001–4,000 ft	4,001–6,000 ft	6,001–8,000 ft

Dial Gauge	Half-Pint or Pint	75	11		12	13	14
Weighted Gauge	Half-Pint or Pint	75	10	15			

Nutrition Facts per Pint

After successfully processing your oysters, you can now serve them to your family at any time. Hence, it is necessary for you to know the nutrition facts for this recipe so that you can adjust the serving or proportion of oysters in your meals. The table below shows the nutrition facts of this recipe in a pint jar:

Nutrition Component	Amount
Calories	154 kcal
Total Fat	5.1 g
Saturated Fat	1.4 g
Carbohydrates	8.1 g
Total Sugars	1.9 g
Sodium	1416 mg
Cholesterol	121 mg
Protein	17.1 g
Calcium	179 mg
Potassium	468 mg
Iron	14 mg

With these instructions in hand, you're ready to preserve and savor the taste of oysters whenever the craving strikes! As always, safety is paramount, so ensure you adhere to all guidelines. Enjoy!

CRABS

Crab is a very well-loved seafood. In fact, it is very common to see people post about their crab meals and cravings. Truth be told, I also enjoy eating crabs. I consume it as part of my feel-good meal. If you or any family member also eats crabs as part of your emotional support meal, then I highly suggest that you learn this canned crab meat recipe. The recipe I use makes use of king and dungeness crab meat. Meanwhile, if you are thinking of canning blue crab meat, it is recommended that you freeze this meat instead for the best quality. This recipe I am using was adopted from the National Institute of Food and Agriculture. It is stated that crab meat processed according to these canning guidelines may result in an acidic flavor. If you don't want such flavor, opt for freezing your crabs instead.

Time: Varies (depends on the number of crabs)

Serving Size: 1 pint (Nutrition calculated per pint)

Yield: Varies (based on the number of crabs)

Prep Time: 60 minutes

Processing Time: Varies based on guidelines

Description:

Crab meat, a fan favorite for many, is easily canned for a delectable meal at any time. This recipe focuses on preserving the rich flavor of king and dungeness crabs. To maintain the meat's texture and quality, consider the note on blue crab meat.

Compared to other seafood recipes, this one has a longer list of ingredients than the rest. Yet it has similar preparation and processing steps. Don't get overwhelmed with the list of ingredients. For example, this recipe is also processed in either half-pint or pint jars, and the crabs must be left on ice while waiting to be prepared and processed. By following the guidelines closely, you can surely preserve your crab meat and have a readily available supply of this recipe at any time.

Skill Level: Intermediate

Special Equipment: Canner

Safety Considerations:

- Always follow food safety standards.

- Be cautious about dietary restrictions when serving.

Ingredients:

- King or Dungeness Crabs

- Lemon Juice

- Citric Acid

- Water

- Salt

- White Vinegar

Directions:

1. **Crab Preparation:** Thoroughly wash the crabs in multiple batches of cold water.

2. **Simmering:** Place crabs in a pot, adding water, 1 cup of lemon juice per gallon, and 2 tablespoons of salt per gallon. Let it simmer for 20 minutes.

3. **Cooling and Meat Extraction:** Cool the crabs in cold water and drain. Remove the back shell and extract meat from the body and claws.

4. **Meat Soaking:** Prepare a solution of cold water, 2 tablespoons of salt per gallon, either 2 cups of lemon juice or 4 cups of vinegar per gallon. Soak the crab meat for 2 minutes.

5. **Draining:** Drain the meat, ensuring you squeeze out excess moisture.

6. **Jar Filling:** Fill pint jars with 340 g of crab meat (170 g for half-pint jars), ensuring a 1-inch headspace.

7. **Acidifying and Sealing:** Add 1 teaspoon of citric acid or 4 tablespoons of lemon juice to a pint jar. Cover with boiling water, preserving a 1-inch headspace.

8. **Final Touches**: Debubble jars, wipe the rims with a damp paper towel, adjust lids, and process as per canning guidelines.

The steps above are tedious tasks. Hence, if you have accomplished each step successfully, it would be a waste if you did not follow the recommended time and pressure. To avoid that and to ensure that the crab meat you will serve to your family is safe for consumption, follow the table below:

Type of Canner	Jar Size	Process Time (in minutes)	Canner Pressure (in lb)				
			0–1,000 ft	1,001–2,000 ft	2,001–4,000 ft	4,001–6,000 ft	6,001–8,000 ft
Dial Gauge	Half-Pint	70	11		12	13	14
	Pint	80	11		12	13	14
Weighted Gauge	Half-Pint	70	10	15			
	Pint	80	10	15			

Nutrition Facts per Pint

Now, you need to know the nutrition facts per pint of this recipe. Adjust how much of a serving size or proportion each member of your family eats. In addition, be careful with any dietary restrictions. The table below will guide you in determining your serving size:

Nutrition Component	Amount
Calories	1004 kcal
Total Fat	16.2 g
Saturated Fat	1.9 g
Carbohydrates	1.3 g
Total Sugars	1.3 g

Nutrition Component	Amount
Sodium	9668 mg
Cholesterol	541 mg
Protein	197.9 g
Calcium	614 mg
Potassium	2751 mg
Iron	8 mg

Enjoy this rich, flavorsome canned crab meat with your loved ones! Always prioritize safety and be aware of dietary restrictions when serving.

SMOKED FISH

Who says you can't smoke fish? You can get creative by canning smoked fish. This pressure-canned smoked fish recipe I will share with you works for smoked salmon, flatfish, and rockfish. In addition, this recipe only requires you to lightly smoke your fish to enhance the flavor, and the flesh will become drier after processing. You should be careful with this recipe. You should also not use this recipe with other smoked seafoods, as the safe processing times for smoked seafoods have yet to be studied. Another safety precaution is not to taste lightly smoked fish since it is not fully cooked yet.

Time: Varies (depends on the amount of fish and smoking duration)

Serving Size: 1 pint (Nutrition calculated per pint)

Yield: Varies (based on the amount of fish)

Prep Time: 45 minutes

Processing Time: Varies based on guidelines

Description:

Elevate the flavors of your fish by trying this pressure-canned smoked fish recipe, suitable for salmon, flatfish, and rockfish. While the smoking is light and enhances the flavor, remember that the fish will be drier post-processing. Safety is paramount: do not taste lightly smoked fish as it's not fully cooked.

Skill Level: Intermediate

Special Equipment: 16- to 22-quart Pressure Canner

Safety Considerations:

- Only use this method for smoked salmon, flatfish, and rockfish.

- Ensure fish is lightly smoked and not fully cooked before canning.

- Always prioritize safety when handling seafood.

Ingredients:

- Lightly smoked fish (e.g., salmon)

Yes, that's just one ingredient. For my personal recipe, I like using smoked salmon. Yet, you should be careful with the processing of smoked fish. First, only process your smoked fish in a 16- to 22-quart pressure canner. Do not attempt to use smaller canners, especially smaller pressure saucepans. It is recommended to use pint jars in processing smoked fish, although you can use half-pints, but the quality may suffer.

Directions:

1. **Thawing**: Ensure that your smoked fish, if previously frozen, is completely thawed and free of ice crystals.

2. **Preparation**: Cut the smoked fish into smaller pieces suitable for pint jars.

3. **Jar Filling**: Pack the fish vertically into your jars, ensuring a 1-inch headspace. You can opt for a tight or loose packing.

4. **No Liquids**: Do not add water or other liquids to the jars.

5. **Final Touches**: Debubble the jars, wipe off any excess food on the rims, and adjust the lids. Your fish is now ready for processing.

6. **Canner Preparation**: Add four quarts of cool tap water to your pressure canner. The water might reach the screw bands of the jars, but don't reduce the amount. Start with cool water and do not preheat before beginning the processing.

To safely process your smoked fish, follow the table below for the recommended time and pressure:

Type of Canner	Jar Size	Process Time (in minutes)	Canner Pressure (in lb)				
			0–1,000 ft	1,001–2,000 ft	2,001–4,000 ft	4,001–6,000 ft	6,001–8,000 ft
Dial Gauge	Pint	110	11		12	13	14
Weighted Gauge	Pint	110	10	15			

Nutrition Facts per Pint

If you have successfully recreated this recipe, you should know how much of a serving size or proportion of this canned smoked fish you and your family should eat during your meal. The table below shows the nutrition facts for a pint jar-serving of this recipe. Adjust your serving size accordingly.

Nutrition Component	Amount
Calories	351 kcal
Total Fat	13 g
Saturated Fat	2.8 g
Carbohydrates	0 g
Total Sugars	0 g
Sodium	2352 mg
Cholesterol	69 mg
Protein	54.8 g
Calcium	33 mg
Potassium	525 mg
Iron	3 mg

Experience a different side of seafood with this delightful canned smoked fish. Always be conscious of safety guidelines and enjoy!

SALMON

In the last recipe, I told you that I prefer to use salmon in my canned smoked fish recipe. This is because I personally like the taste and flavor of salmon. It is also an easy fish to cook. I also noticed that my family likes eating salmon compared to other kinds of fish. I also enjoy preparing and cooking salmon. It feels like art to me. If you are fond of salmon too, then you might as well try to learn this recipe. You will surely be thrilled that you have a readily available supply of salmon at any day or time, even during emergencies. In fact, during the COVID-19 lockdown, my family and I were lucky to have a lot of canned salmon in our pantry, which became part of our meal every time we wanted to destress.

The recipe does not end with the gathering of ingredients. You need to prepare and process them too. I really like preparing salmon. Although you can process your salmon, either hot-packed or raw-packed, I prefer to prepare them hot-packed. This is because I enjoy precooking it. I bake my salmon only until it is lightly cooked. You can adopt this too.

Time: Varies (depends on the amount of salmon and cooking duration)

Serving Size: 1 pint (Nutrition calculated per pint)

Yield: 10 pint jars

Prep Time: 45 minutes

Processing Time: Varies based on guidelines

Description:

Salmon is a universally loved fish with a unique and delightful flavor. This canned salmon recipe ensures you have a delicious source of protein on hand anytime. The preparation feels like an art, and the result is an ever-ready supply of this delectable fish.

Skill Level: Intermediate

Special Equipment: Canning jars and equipment

Safety Considerations:

- Ensure proper sterilization of jars and lids.

- Make sure the fish is fresh or properly thawed if frozen.

Ingredients:

- Salmon: 1.8 kg

- Salt: 1/2 teaspoon per pint jar

- Vinegar (optional): 1/2 teaspoon per pint jar

Directions:

1. **Fileting**: Start by preparing your salmon. Filet the fish. You can opt to leave or remove the skin and bones. Once fileted, cut the salmon into smaller chunks or strips to fit into the canning jars.

2. **Packing Method**: Decide between raw-packing or hot-packing. For hot-packing, lightly precook the salmon until it's partially done. Fill your jars with salmon, packing them tightly. Ensure a 1-inch headspace and add salt as desired.

3. **Vinegar Addition**: While adding cooking liquid isn't necessary, vinegar can be added. It helps in softening the bones. Incorporate 1/2 teaspoon of vinegar for each pint jar if desired.

4. **Final Touches**: Debubble the jars and wipe the rims using a damp paper towel. Adjust the lids, and your salmon is now prepared for the canning process.

To ensure that your canned salmon will remain safe for consumption even after several months, follow the table below for the recommended processing time and pressure:

Type of Canner	Jar Size	Process Time (in minutes)	Canner Pressure (in lb)				
			0–1,000 ft	1,001–2,000 ft	2,001–4,000 ft	4,001–6,000 ft	6,001–8,000 ft
Dial Gauge	Pint	110	11		12	13	14
Weighted Gauge	Pint	110	10	15			

Nutrition Facts per Pint

Now that you can successfully process canned salmon, it is time to learn its nutrition facts. You need this so you can adjust the serving size or proportion of canned salmon according to your dietary needs. The table below shows the nutrition facts for a pint jar:

Nutrition Component	Amount
Calories	1489 kcal
Total Fat	34.8 g
Saturated Fat	7.2 g
Carbohydrates	0 g
Total Sugars	0 g
Sodium	3083 mg
Cholesterol	828 mg
Protein	295.2 g
Calcium	121 mg
Potassium	5450 mg
Iron	7 mg

This canned salmon recipe is perfect for those who appreciate the fine taste of salmon and want to ensure they have a supply on hand. The process is both rewarding and enjoyable, giving you a delicious result every time!

Chapter 10

OTHER PRESSURE CANNING RECIPES TO TRY

You now know various pressure canning recipes, such as meat, vegetable, and soup recipes. Yet, it is better if you learn more. After all, one of the goals is to build or collect a number of canned foods for daily consumption and emergencies. Hence, it will be beneficial for you if you add more variations to your pantry stock. Some of the recipes I would like to share with you are salsa, spaghetti sauce, and tomato juice. Such recipes will allow you to have a readily available supply for any quick recipes you want on days when you are too busy to cook food from scratch.

SALSA

This recipe will truly be enjoyed by people with a home garden. Or you may be someone who does not know what to do with their tomatoes, peppers, onions, and jalapenos. Or you may be someone who just enjoys eating food with salsa. For me, I always have canned salsa stock in my pantry. This is because I enjoy eating snacks, specifically chips. I always dip my chips with salsa, thus the uncountable number of canned salsas in my pantry. If you enjoy dipping your chips in salsa too, or if you like eating tacos, then this recipe is perfect for you. Now, if you are someone who wants to can their own salsa, here is a recipe I will share with you.

You can adjust the proportions of the seasonings according to your liking. This recipe is easy and beginner-friendly. The preparation for this recipe is pretty straightforward and requires hot packing

Time: Varies (depends on simmering duration)

Serving Size: 1 pint (Nutrition calculated per pint)

Yield: 4 pint jars

Prep Time: 30 minutes

Processing Time: Varies based on guidelines

Description:

For salsa enthusiasts, gardeners, or those with a penchant for chips and tacos, this salsa recipe ensures you have a tasty condiment on hand anytime. Canning salsa provides a delightful, homemade flavor that's hard to match with store-bought versions.

Skill Level: Beginner

Special Equipment: Canning jars and equipment, large pot, saucepan

Safety Considerations:

- Ensure proper sterilization of jars and lids.

- Use fresh produce to ensure quality and safety.

Ingredients:

- Tomatoes: 2 kg

- Onions: 6 pieces

- Garlic: 4 cloves

- Jalapeno peppers: 2 pieces

- Hot pepper sauce (optional): 2 tablespoons

- White vinegar: 1/2 cup

- Lime juice: 2 tablespoons

- Cilantro: 2 tablespoons

- Salt: 2 teaspoons

Directions:

1. **Preparation**: Begin by washing the tomatoes and peppers. For the tomatoes, blanch them briefly in hot water until their skins start to peel. Cool them quickly

in an ice bath and then peel off the skins. Chop or press the tomatoes to your desired consistency.

2. **Chopping**: Dice your onions, jalapenos, and garlic.

3. **Cooking**: In a large pot, combine the chopped tomatoes, onions, jalapenos, garlic, and the rest of the ingredients. Simmer the mixture until it reaches your preferred consistency and heat level.

4. **Jarring**: Pour the hot salsa into preheated canning jars, maintaining a 1/2-inch headspace.

5. **Finishing**: Debubble the jars, wipe the rims clean, adjust the lids, and prepare your salsa for the canning process.

To process your salsa, there are recommended times and conditions that you must follow. These are provided in the table below:

Type of Canner	Jar Size	Process Time (in minutes)	Canner Pressure (in lb)				
			0–1,000 ft	1,001–2,000 ft	2,001–4,000 ft	4,001–6,000 ft	6,001–8,000 ft
Dial Gauge	Pint	10	11		12	13	14
	Quart	15	11		12	13	14
Weighted Gauge	Pint	10	10	15			
	Quart	15	10	15			

Nutrition Facts per Pint

After processing your salsa, you should know how much of it you and your family can eat during snacks for chips or meals for tacos. The table below shows the nutrition facts per pint jar:

Nutrition Component	Amount
Calories	171 kcal
Total Fat	1.3 g
Saturated Fat	0.2 g
Carbohydrates	37.1 g
Total Sugars	20.6 g
Sodium	1380 mg
Cholesterol	0 mg
Protein	6.5 g
Calcium	100 mg
Potassium	1490 mg
Iron	2 mg

With this recipe, you can enjoy fresh, homemade salsa anytime you like. Perfect for snacks, meals, and a great way to preserve the bounty from your garden.

SPAGHETTI SAUCE

Spaghetti is an easy meal to eat. It is a nice meal that everyone, regardless of age, can enjoy. To add variety to your pantry stock, pressure can spaghetti sauces. As long as you don't add noodles or any thickening agents, your pressure-canned sauces can surely remain consumable even after several months. This is my favorite spaghetti sauce recipe: a bolognese-style spaghetti sauce with ground meat. This recipe makes use of hot packing.

Time: About 3 hours

Serving Size: 1 pint (Nutrition calculated per pint)

Yield: 9 pint jars

Prep Time: 45 minutes

Processing Time: Varies based on guidelines

Description:

Spaghetti is a universal comfort food loved by all ages. Enhance your pantry collection with this pressure-canned bolognese-style spaghetti sauce. The absence of noodles and thickening agents ensures longevity, making this a perfect meal even after several months.

Skill Level: Intermediate

Special Equipment: Canning jars and equipment, pot, skillet, sieve

Safety Considerations:

- Ensure the jars and lids are properly sterilized.
- Avoid adding noodles or thickening agents.

Ingredients:

- Tomatoes: 14 kg
- Onion: 175 g
- Ground beef: 1 kg
- Garlic: 5 cloves
- Mushrooms: 500 g
- Dried oregano: 2 tablespoons

- Dried parsley: 1 tablespoon
- Salt: 1 tablespoon
- Brown sugar: 4 teaspoons
- Ground black pepper: 2 teaspoons

Directions:

1. **Tomato Preparation**: Hull and peel the tomatoes, then quarter them.
2. **Veggie Chopping**: Dice the onions, garlic, and mushrooms.
3. **Tomato Boiling**: Place tomatoes in a pot and boil for 20 minutes. Press the boiled tomatoes through a sieve.
4. **Beef Browning**: Brown the ground beef in a skillet for about 3-5 minutes, or until it starts releasing its juice.
5. **Veggie Sautéing**: Add onions and mushrooms to the skillet, stirring often until the mushrooms shrink and onions become translucent.
6. **Mix & Simmer**: Add all seasonings and pressed tomatoes to the skillet. Bring to a boil, then simmer uncovered for 2-3 hours.
7. **Canning**: Pour hot sauce into preheated canning jars, ensuring a 1-inch headspace. Debubble, clean the rims, adjust the lids, and process.

Before you can stock your canned spaghetti sauce, you need to process it first in a pressure canner. You need to know the processing time and pressure that you need. The table below will serve as your guide:

Type of Canner	Jar Size	Process Time (in minutes)	Canner Pressure (in lb)				
			0–1,000 ft	1,001–2,000 ft	2,001–4,000 ft	4,001–6,000 ft	6,001–8,000 ft
Dial Gauge	Pint	60	11		12	13	14
	Quart	70	11		12	13	14
Weighted Gauge	Pint	60	10	15			
	Quart	70	10	15			

Nutrition Facts per Pint

Now that you know how to can this spaghetti sauce recipe, you need to know how much of it you can serve to your family. To guide you in determining the appropriate serving size for each family member, refer to the table below. This table shows the nutrition facts for a pint jar:

Nutrition Component	Amount
Calories	266 kcal
Total Fat	7.5 g
Saturated Fat	2.7 g
Carbohydrates	12.5 g
Total Sugars	7.2 g
Sodium	861 mg
Cholesterol	99 mg
Protein	37.3 g
Calcium	44 mg
Potassium	1055 mg
Iron	24 mg

Enjoy the deliciousness of homemade spaghetti sauce with this recipe. Perfect for family dinners, gatherings, or simply when you're in the mood for a comforting pasta dish.

TOMATO JUICE

Tomato juice is a versatile ingredient in various recipes. This can be a great addition to your prepper pantry. This is a beginner-friendly recipe. In fact, this is one of the first recipes I learned when I was still learning how to pressure can.

Time: Approximately 1 hour

Serving Size: 1 pint (Nutrition calculated per pint)

Yield: 9 pint jars

Prep Time: 15 minutes

Processing Time: Varies based on guidelines

Description:

Tomato juice is a staple ingredient in many recipes and an excellent addition to any pantry. Even for beginners, this is a straightforward pressure-canning recipe, perfect for those just getting started with home preservation.

Skill Level: Beginner

Special Equipment: Canning jars and equipment, saucepan, sieve

Safety Considerations:

- Always acidify your tomato juice to ensure safe canning.

- Sterilize jars and lids before use.

Ingredients:

- Tomatoes: 6 kg

- Lemon juice: 1 tablespoon per pint OR Citric acid: 1/4 teaspoon per pint

- Salt: 1/2 teaspoon per pint

Directions:

1. **Tomato Preparation**: Wash the tomatoes, remove stems, and discard any bruised or discolored spots. Quarter the tomatoes.

2. **Boil & Crush**: In a saucepan, start with a batch of quartered tomatoes. As they begin boiling, crush them and gradually add in the remaining tomatoes. Ensure a constant boil and simmer for 5 minutes after all tomatoes are added.

3. **Strain**: Push the tomato juice through a sieve to remove skins and seeds.

4. **Acidify**: Add lemon juice or citric acid per the given measurements.

5. **Re-Boil**: Bring the juice back to a boil.

6. **Canning**: Pour the tomato juice into preheated canning jars, leaving a 0.5-inch headspace. Debubble jars, clean the rims, adjust the lids, and process.

To ensure that your tomato juice is safe for consumption, refer to the table below for the processing time and pressure needed.

Type of Canner	Jar Size	Process Time (in minutes)	Canner Pressure (in lb)				
			0–1,000 ft	1,001–2,000 ft	2,001–4,000 ft	4,001–6,000 ft	6,001–8,000 ft
Dial Gauge	Pint	20	6		7	8	9
	Quart	15	11		12	13	14
Weighted Gauge	Pint	20	5	10			
	Quart	15	10	15			

Nutrition Facts per Pint

Now, it is time for you to determine the nutrition facts for this recipe. Adjust your serving proportions according to the table below, which shows the nutrition facts for a pint jar.

Nutrition Component	Amount
Calories	123 kcal
Total Fat	1.4 g
Saturated Fat	0.2 g
Carbohydrates	26.9 g
Total Sugars	17.9 g
Sodium	1198 mg
Cholesterol	0 mg
Protein	5.9 g
Calcium	69 mg
Potassium	1596 mg
Iron	2 mg

This simple yet versatile tomato juice is perfect for various culinary applications, from making soups to flavoring dishes or even drinking straight for a nutritious boost. Enjoy!

Conclusion

MASTERING THE ART OF PRESSURE CANNING

As a homesteader, you will surely love and enjoy how pressure canning can bring your preserved food to your table year-round. Pressure canning is a great skill to learn. It will allow you to process your own foods. You can be flexible and creative with your recipes. You can also ensure that what you feed your family is healthy and made of quality ingredients without added preservatives. Pressure canning also allows you to preserve foods that do not contain enough acid to kill harmful bacteria, such as botulism.

I am really positive that you will enjoy processing your own foods. You can also ensure that the ingredients you add are only those that you will eat. Pressure canning your food is a safe way to preserve it. I would like to emphasize that the previous sentence is true as long as you follow safety precautions, guidelines, and the recommended processing time and pressure.

Food processing will teach you a lot about food, your body, health, and even heat and pressure. It will even allow you to build enough knowledge to establish your daily and emergency pantries. Your family will surely feel lucky and love seeing your efforts in processing and preserving healthy and delicious meals in jars. You just need to be careful with the risks associated with pressure canning. Included in these risks are the proper preparation and processing to kill harmful bacteria and ensuring that you get the right altitude for your location so you can properly operate your pressure canner.

Never forget the necessary safety tips that you have learned in this book. I hope that you always remember to add headspace, not reuse lids, clean the rims of the jars before adjusting lids, and remove air bubbles before processing. Such small details can hinder the preservation and sealing of your jars. Once you notice that your canned jars did not seal properly after 12 to 24 hours of processing, either reprocess or refrigerate the canned foods. As I often emphasize, always prioritize your and your family's safety when it comes to food consumption.

I have shared a lot of recipes with you through this book. You now know how to pressure can poultry, meat, seafood, vegetables, stock, soup, salsa, spaghetti sauce, and tomato juice. With all the recipes you can process, you will surely need to establish a prepper pantry, both for your daily meals and emergency needs. Remember the tips I shared with you with regards to a prepper pantry, including planning your meals, tracking your inventory, and making sure that your pantry area provides a cool, dry place for your canned foods?

I am so happy to be able to share with you the knowledge I have gained over the past several years. I have truly loved pressure canning and processing our own foods. I have also genuinely enjoyed writing this book while thinking about the skills you will learn. I am excited for your journey. I hope that I have provided you with all the know-how of pressure canning.

References

Adamant, A. (2020, November 5). *12 common beginner canning mistakes (and how to fix them)*. Practical Self Reliance. https://practicalselfreliance.com/beginner-canning-mistakes/

Adamant, A. (2021, January 25). *Canning beef*. Practical Self Reliance. https://practicalselfreliance.com/canning-beef/

Adamant, A. (2022, November 8). *Canning chicken soup*. Practical Self reliance. https://creativecanning.com/canning-chicken-soup/

Blair, C. (n.d.). *What foods can & cannot be pressure canned: Complete list*. EZ-Prepping. https://ezprepping.com/what-foods-can-and-cannot-be-pressure-canned-complete-list/

Canning beef pot roast. (n.d.). Healthy Canning. https://www.healthycanning.com/canning-beef-pot-roast

Canning beef short rib. (n.d.). Healthy canning. https://www.healthycanning.com/canning-beef-short-rib

Canning beef stew. (2021, June 2). Creative Homemaking. https://creativehomemaking.com/recipes/canning/how-to-can-beef-stew/

Canning chicken stock. (n.d.). Healthy Canning. https://www.healthycanning.com/canning-chicken-stock

Canning pork. (n.d.). Healthy Canning. https://www.healthycanning.com/canning-pork

Canning pulled shredded pork. (n.d.). SB Canning. https://www.sbcanning.com/2013/11/canning-pulled-shredded-pork.html

Chicken and gravy dinner in a jar. (n.d.). Healthy Canning. https://www.healthycanning.com/chicken-gravy-dinner-jar

Complete guide to home canning. (n.d.). National Institute of Food and Agriculture.https://nchfp.uga.edu/publications/usda/GUIDE01_HomeCan_rev0715.pdf

Creating a prepper food pantry - the step by step guide. (n.d.). Backdoor Prepper. https://backdoorprepper.com/creating-a-prepper-food-pantry-the-step-by-step-guide

Durand, F. (2019, June 5). *15 tips for better weekly meal planning.* The Kitchn. https://www.thekitchn.com/10-tips-for-better-weekly-meal-planning-reader-intelligence-report-177252

Food preservation quotes. (n.d.). Quotlr. https://quotlr.com/quotes-about-food-preservation

Geiger, M. (2021, August 17). *Potential deadly canning mistakes.* Iowa State University. https://blogs.extension.iastate.edu/answerline/2021/08/17/potentially-deadly-canning-mistakes/

Hoory, L. (2021, November 11). *The key differences between natural and artificial food preservatives — and what it means for your health.* Insider. https://www.insider.com/guides/health/diet-nutrition/what-are-preservatives

How to use a pressure canner safely. (n.d.). The House & Homestead. https://thehouseandhomestead.com/how-to-use-a-pressure-canner-safely/

King, C. (n.d.). *Canning salmon.* Canned Nation. https://cannednation.com/canning-salmon/?expand_article=1#google_vignette

Lai, O. (2021, November 22). *What is food waste.* Earth Org. https://earth.org/what-is-food-waste/

99+ world food safety day quotes. (n.d.). Captions Book. https://captionsbook.com/world-food-safety-day-quotes/

Pazzaglia, L. (2018, May 24). *Pressure canning guide & FAQ: Put 'em up!* Hip Pressure Cooking. https://www.hippressurecooking.com/pressure-canning-faq-put-em-up/#exh

Phelan, K. (n.d.). *4 canning dangers to be aware of.* Homestead Survival Site. https://homesteadsurvivalsite.com/canning-dangers/

Pierce, R. (2023, March 6). *How to pressure can salsa step by step.* New Life on a Homestead. https://www.newlifeonahomestead.com/how-to-can-salsa/

Preserving food….lentil soup, thm e, gluten free, sugar free. (2020, September 16). Around the Family Table Blog. https://aroundthefamilytableblog.com/2020/09/16/preserving-food-lentil-soup-thm-e-gluten-free-sugar-free/

Pressure canning altitude chart. (n.d.). Pressure Canners. https://pressurecanners.com/pressure-canning-altitude-chart/

Pressure canning shrimp instructions. (n.d.). The Canning Diva. https://www.canningdiva.com/recipes/pressure-canning-shrimp-instructions/

Principles of pressure canning. (n.d.). Utah State University. https://extension.usu.edu/preserve-the-harvest/research/principles-of-pressure-canning

Singh, R.P., & Desrosier, N.W. (2023, August 8). *Food preservation.* https://www.britannica.com/topic/food-preservation

Spaghetti sauce with meat. (n.d.). Healthy Canning. https://www.healthycanning.com/spaghetti-sauce-with-meat

The history of home canning and preserving food. (n.d.). Canning Diva. https://www.canningdiva.com/the-history-of-home-canning-and-preserving-food/

The sustainable development goals report 2023. (n.d.). United Nations.https://www.un.org/sustainabledevelopment/hunger/

The ultimate list of what you can (and cannot!) can. (n.d.). J&R Pierce Family Farm. https://www.jrpiercefamilyfarm.com/blog-1/2019/08/15/the-ultimate-list-of-what-you-can-and-cannot-can

Vegetable soup for canning up your garden. (n.d.). SB Canning. https://www.sbcanning.com/2014/01/vegetable-soup-for-canning-up-your.html

Water Bath Canning

&

Preserving for Beginners

A Step-By-Step Guide To Start Your Own Preservative-Free Prepper Pantry - Featuring 55 Starter Recipes To Can Fruits, Vegetables, Jams, Sauces, And More

Elizabeth Ash

Introduction

The Wonders of Water Bath Canning

Have you ever seen a prepper pantry?

You know, one of those storage spaces that is filled with cans, bottles, and boxes of preserved food and other essential items. Having such a room at home will make you feel more confident about your safety in case something unexpected occurs.

Building your own prepper pantry might seem like an overwhelming task, but it doesn't have to be. As long as you have extra space in your home, you can start filling it with essential items.

These days, there is a lot of uncertainty. The world is constantly changing and we constantly hear devastating news about natural disasters and other unexpected tragedies. Such news often comes with feelings of fear, especially if you know that you aren't ready to deal with situations like those. Some of the most common worrisome thoughts that may have gone through your mind include:

- That the food you have at home will go bad, thus rendering it inedible.
- Power outages that last for a long time will cause your stocked freezer meals and other frozen products to go bad.

- All the money you have spent on food will go to waste.
- There will be food shortages, which means that you won't even get a chance to buy food even if you have the money for it.
- The only foods available will contain a lot of chemicals and preservatives, and eating too much of these could contribute to the development of health issues.

When you're already struggling in the midst of a natural disaster, having to deal with these things will make life even more difficult for you. Fortunately, you can easily calm your mind by starting to build your own prepper pantry.Stock your pantry with healthy, tasty foods that you have made yourself. Preserving your own foods at home is highly recommended when building a prepper pantry. And when it comes to preserving food, one of the easiest and most wonderful ways to do this is through water bath canning.

Water bath canning is a type of preservation method. The process involves canning high-acid foods in glass jars. This is a very easy process where you fill jars with food, seal them with lids, then boil the jars for specific amounts of time in order to maintain the quality of the food stored inside. It's such a simple process that you can easily do it at home. High-acid foods include fruits, jellies, jams, relishes, pickled vegetables, and more.

If you have never tried home canning before, it's recommended to start with water bath canning because of the simplicity of the process. When I became interested in food preservation, I started with this process too.

I learned all about water canning through my grandmother. In fact, I learned all about food preservation and building a prepper pantry from my grandmother too. Whenever I visited her home, I was fascinated with this one room where she kept different kinds of food. When I was young, I used to sneak into that room often just to stare at all the jars and bottles.

As I grew older, my grandmother introduced me to the importance of having food stores at home. At first, I didn't really take her seriously. But then, the more I thought about it, the more I realized that having a prepper pantry made a lot of sense. So my husband and I started learning more about it. We started with water bath canning as this process was something my grandmother had been doing since she was young.

When she found out that we wanted to preserve our own food, she passed down her secrets to us. Since then, we have been canning our own food at home. Now, we have a fully-stocked prepper pantry that keeps us feeling safe, food-wise even if something unexpected were to happen. We have gotten so good at preserving different kinds of food that we even give them out as gifts, which always brings a smile to the faces of our friends and loved ones.

To take things even further, we have decided to write this book to share what we know about water bath canning with anyone who is interested. The great thing about this process is that it's one of the most popular and easiest ways to preserve different types of food. Water bath canning is an easy process, which you can master given the right knowledge. And you don't even need any special equipment for it.

Water bath canning is recommended by modern homesteaders because of its convenience and simplicity. Once you master this process, then you can start learning how to preserve food through other processes too. Although this process might seem intimidating, especially if you haven't tried home canning before, you don't have to worry.

From defining the process, explaining how it works, and what are the benefits you can gain from it, there is much for you to learn. By the end of this book, you will have a thorough understanding of what water bath canning is all about. You can even start canning foods at home since this book also contains lots of recipes to get you started. So if you're ready to start learning, turn the page, and let's begin!

Chapter 1

WATER BATH CANNING BASICS

Simply put, water bath canning is a process where you preserve food by placing it into a jar, then immersing it in a hot water bath. It's important to place the food in hot jars that you have already sterilized. Placing the jars in boiling water kills off the bacteria that cause foods to spoil. This process also sucks out the air from inside the jars, which then allows the lids to seal the jars tightly. This is important so that the food inside the jars stays shelf-stable.

One of the best things about water bath canning is that it's a very simple process. You can invest in a water bath canner, but a large stockpot would work just as well. As long as you know how the process works, you will be able to preserve many types of food through water bath canning.

How Does Water Bath Canning Work?

Simple as this process is, it's very good at preserving certain types of food. Water bath canning is so effective because it kills bacteria and sucks out the air from the jars to prevent the growth of new bacteria. Both processes prevent the food inside the jars from getting spoiled. The process works this way:

- You preheat your water bath canner with the jars inside in order to sterilize them. You can sterilize the jars separately too.
- After sterilizing the jars, you pack the food inside along with any liquid you would use to preserve the food.
- Once you immerse the jars inside the water bath canner, the high temperature of the water sucks out the air from the foods and the jar itself.
- A vacuum is created inside the jar, which then causes the lid to seal the jars tightly.

You must make sure that the rims and lids are very clean before you place the jars in the canner. Do this by using a paper towel to wipe the rims before screwing the lids on tightly. Water bath canning is only suitable for high-acid foods. It's also possible to can low-acid foods, but you need to acidify them first through pickling or some other safe process. If you plan to do this, it's important for you to follow the recipes carefully to ensure that you preserve the foods safely.

If you want to start preserving foods through water bath canning, you don't need a specialized canning pot for this purpose. You can use any stockpot that's big and deep enough to place your jars. It's also important for the canner (or pot) to have a lid to ensure that the water inside the pot boils continuously throughout the processing time.

Once in a while, the jars might break while you are processing them inside the canner. If this happens, gently take the broken jars out of the canner along with the contents. At this point, you can continue processing the other jars. As for the broken jars, discard them along with all of their contents.

How Does Water Bath Canning Differ From Other Food Preservation Methods

Water bath canning isn't the only food preservation method out there. But since it's the easiest, it's recommended to start with this one. To help you understand this process better, let's take a look at the different methods of canning. This will also help you understand what sets water bath canning apart from the other processes.

Water Bath Canning

For this process, the jars placed inside the water bath canner are surrounded by boiling water. To ensure that the process works correctly, you need to make sure that the canner contains enough boiling water to surround the jars completely. You also need to place a rack inside the pot rather than placing the jars directly into the bottom of the pot. This allows water to circulate underneath the jars while processing.

There should also be enough space on top of the pot to ensure that the water level is at least two inches above the jars. You can either purchase a water bath canner and think of it as an investment or you can work with a pot that you already have at home, at least at the beginning. Just make sure that the pot is big enough for the jars you will process. For instance, if your pot is a bit small, you need to buy jars that are a bit small too. That way, they can fit inside the pot for proper processing.

Water bath canning is suitable for most types of fruits, jams, jellies, pickles, and other high-acid foods. Simplicity is one of the features that sets this process apart, which is why it's perfect for those who want to learn how to preserve foods through canning without any previous experience. It's also ideal because you don't need to have special equipment in order to start canning your own food at home.

Atmospheric Steam Canning

This is a recently developed canning method that can be used for food preservation at home. For this, you will need an atmospheric steam canner. This process is also suitable for high-acid foods. Atmospheric steam canners have a low base, a tall lid, and a rack for placing the jars. The lid has a special design with holes near the base. The holes allow the steam to escape during the canning process.

When processing jars with food in this type of canner, you need to keep the lid on throughout the process. Since an atmospheric steam canner works the same way as a water bath canner, processing times are usually the same. However, if you need to process foods for more than 45 minutes, you shouldn't use this process as the water in the canner might evaporate completely before reaching the proper processing time.

Pressure Canning

Pressure canning is the only suitable method for canning low-acid foods like most vegetables, meat, poultry, seafood, and more. This is the only safe method for canning such foods that doesn't pose a risk of botulism. Since botulism spores can survive temperatures as high as the boiling point of water, canning low-acid foods using steam or water bath canners isn't safe. Pressure canning is your only option.

While processing, the temperature inside a pressure canner gets high enough to eliminate botulism spores, thus making the preserved food safe enough to eat. For this method, you need a pressure canner. This is a specialized piece of equipment, unlike the simple pot that you would need for water bath canning. You need to invest in a pressure canner if you want to preserve your foods using this method. Since it's possible to preserve many other types of food using the water bath canning method, many choose to start with the simple process.

Apart from these three canning methods, there are other methods used a long time ago. Unfortunately, these methods aren't considered safe anymore. Thesy include:

- Using an oven to process jars. This isn't recommended because it may cause the jars to explode. Even if they remain intact, ovens won't heat the contents of the jars evenly to ensure proper preservation.
- The hot fill or open kettle method where you simply pour hot food into empty jars, then screw the lids immediately. Since the contents of the jars are hot, the heat seals the lids in place. However, this method isn't safe because it doesn't produce enough heat to prevent the contents of the jars from spoiling.
- Some even try canning using dishwashers, slow cookers, microwaves, or crock pots, all of which aren't recommended because of the same reasons as above.

Aside from these methods, it also isn't recommended to use canning chemicals or powders that are supposed to replace the heating process. Canning foods for preservation is a sensitive process that can produce unsafe results if not done correctly, so it's important to only stick with proper canning methods.

BENEFITS OF WATER BATH CANNING

Many modern homesteaders have started preserving foods through water bath canning. This has become a very popular method of canning that will allow you to fill your prepper pantry with healthy, delicious foods. If you're still wondering why you should go with this method, take a look at the many benefits you can look forward to.

It's a Very Simple and Safe Procedure

One of the best benefits of water bath canning is its simplicity. Anyone with a big enough pot at home can do this process. As you will discover later, the recipes for canning foods this way are very easy to do. As long as you follow the steps and processing times correctly, you can produce safely preserved foods to add to your stockpile.

Eliminates Bacteria That Causes Food Spoilage

Although water bath canning won't eliminate botulism spores, it's effective enough to destroy other bacteria that can cause food spoilage. These include Listeria monocytogenesm, Salmonella enterica, Escherichia coli O157:H7, and more. Again, you can only gain this benefit if you make sure to follow the proper water bath canning procedures, both for high-acid foods and for low-acid foods that you cook or process first before preserving them in your water bath canner.

Allows You to Preserve Certain Low-Acid Foods Through Proper Processing

Speaking of low-acid foods, you can preserve some of these too. But before doing this, you need to either cook the foods first or pickle them, such as in the case of most vegetables. After cooking, processing the foods inside the jars through water bath canning further drives acids into the foods. This, in turn, strengthens the preservation process, which makes even low-acid foods safe for long-term storage.

Creates a Vacuum Inside the Jars to Keep the Contents Preserved

Over time, oxygen causes the degradation of food in terms of nutrition, appearance, and flavor. This is a process that occurs naturally when foods are exposed to oxygen. Since water bath canning sucks out the air from the jars and the foods themselves, it creates a vacuum inside the jars to preserve the contents. When this happens, the lids seal the jars tightly, which prevents air from re-entering the jars until you open them for consumption.

Ensures a Long Shelf-Life

Since water bath canning preserves the contents of the jars, you can store them for months or even years after processing. This long shelf-life is very important, especially if you're planning to build a prepper pantry at home.

Since water bath canning allows you to preserve fresh ingredients without using unnecessary or artificial ingredients, this process also contributes to a healthier lifestyle. You won't have to rely on processed foods just because they have longer shelf lives. You can start preserving your own fresh, nutritious ingredients to ensure that you can keep eating healthy foods even when disaster strikes.

POSSIBLE RISKS OF WATER BATH CANNING

Although preserving food through a water bath canner is generally safe and simple, it isn't a perfect process. In fact, it can be quite risky if you don't learn how to can foods properly. This is why educating yourself about the process is of the essence. To help you understand everything about water bath canning, let's go through the possible risks that you should look out for.

Contamination Through Unsterilized Tools

One of the biggest risks of water bath canning is contamination. If you don't sterilize the jars and any other tools or equipment you use, you could compromise the safety of the food you preserve. Even if you process the jars correctly, using contaminated tools could result in unsafe outcomes. This is why one of the first steps in any recipe for water bath canning is to sterilize your jars first. This is essential to minimize the risk of bacterial growth or contamination through toxins.

It's not enough to simply wash the jars; you should sterilize them in boiling water for a minimum of 10 minutes. Make sure that all of the tools you use for preparing and cooking the ingredients are clean too. Cleanliness prevents contamination, which ensures the safety of your final products.

Reusing Old Lids

It's possible to reuse canning jars, lids, and rings to store food. But when it comes to canning, it's important to purchase new lids. New lids include rubber rings and they are only suitable for one use when it comes to canning. Reusing lids isn't safe as there is a very big chance that they won't seal properly, which means that the food inside won't be preserved safely. To avoid this, you should mark the lids of your jars before storing them.

That way, you know which lids have already been processed in the water bath canner. Use these for short-term storage of foods.

The Danger of Improperly Canning Low-Acid Foods

In this book, you will find many recipes for preserving foods using a water bath canner. If you have tried all of the recipes in this book and you want to try canning other foods, make sure to find recipes that are meant for water bath canning. This is especially important for low-acid foods. While it's possible to preserve some types of low-acid foods in a water bath canner, you need to follow the correct process to ensure your safety. Also, take note of the foods that can only be canned through a pressure canner. We'll go through these foods in the next chapter.

Botulism

This is the most dangerous risk that could come from water bath canning. If you know how to use your water bath canner properly and you apply your knowledge, there is minimal to no risk of botulism. However, if you don't learn how to preserve food through water bath canning properly, this is one risk that could prove fatal.

The bacteria known as Clostridium botulinum causes botulism. This bacteria can be found in improperly preserved canned or jarred goods. Clostridium botulinum produces toxins that attack your nervous system, causing paralysis or even death. Botulism occurs when preserved foods aren't properly processed or sealed.

The bacteria cannot survive in foods with high acid levels, which is why it's perfectly safe to preserve these types of foods through water bath canning. In order to preserve low-acid foods in the same way, you may need to add lemon juice, vinegar, or some other type of acid to increase the level of acidity and eliminate the risk of botulism. This is why you need to pickle vegetables first before canning them using the water bath method.

Apart from being aware of the potential risks of water bath canning, you should also know how to spot issues after you have processed your food through this method. Do this by testing the lids of the jars after they have cooled down completely. Also, make sure that there are no cracks in any of the jars as these could cause contamination.

When it's time to open the jars so you can consume the contents, make sure that the lids make a popping noise when you unscrew them. If they don't, it's better to discard the jar and its contents. Finally, check the underside of the lids to make sure that there aren't any molds, foam, or any odd liquid on them. If you smell something stinky or moldy after opening the jar, discard it along with all the contents. Keeping all of these things in mind will ensure that you will always be safe when processing and consuming your preserved foods.

Chapter 2

BEST AND WORST FOODS TO PRESERVE THROUGH WATER BATH CANNING

Deciding to create your own prepper pantry at home is a very smart move, especially with all the uncertainties of our world today. Even if nothing bad happens, you will still have peace of mind knowing that food-wise you're ready for anything. Also, you have the option to enjoy the foods you have preserved whenever you want. Then you can simply replace the jars you opened since you already know how the water bath canning process works.

But before you start canning foods at home, you should know which foods you can preserve through this process and which foods to avoid. Once you have this knowledge, you can start planning your ingredients before you visit your local farmer's market.

THE BEST FOODS TO PRESERVE

If it's your first time preserving foods through water bath canning, trying to learn everything you need to know can get quite overwhelming. But if you focus on one aspect of this process at a time, learning becomes much easier. After understanding how the process works, it's time to know which foods you can and cannot preserve through water bath canning. First, let's start with the high-acid foods that can be preserved through this method.

Fruits

Most types of fruits can be processed safely using a water bath. These include citrus fruits, apples, pears, plums, peaches, cherries, berries, and more. It's particularly beneficial to can seasonal fruits so that you can enjoy them all year round. Of course, you can also can the more common fruits just to make sure that you have them in your pantry even if something unexpected happens.

Jams and Jellies

Fruits and vegetables can be made into jams, jellies, preserves, and marmalades so that you can process them through water bath canning. It's easy to do this with high-acid fruits like oranges, berries, pears, and peaches, but you can also do this with low-acid fruits and vegetables. The key here is to add some acid to the mix before cooking them into jams and jellies. If you're not yet sure about canning raw ingredients, you can start with jams and jellies. These are much easier to preserve and they tend to have a longer shelf life. These preserved food items are so delicious, especially when you start with fresh ingredients when making them.

Pickled or Fermented Foods

If you want to stock your pantry with foods that don't contain a lot of sugar, such as jams and jellies, consider making pickled or fermented foods instead. Pickling and fermenting are highly recommended for low-acid vegetables. As you will discover, pickling recipes include a lot of vinegar, which significantly increases the acid content of the foods. The great thing about pickling is that it allows you to preserve many different types of veggies.

Relishes, Chutneys, Pie Fillings, Juices, and More

Relishes and chutneys also contain some type of a high-acid component such as vinegar, citric acid, or lemon juice. This addition allows you to process even low-acid ingredients using your water bath canner. Having relishes and chutneys at home allows you to pair these tasty treats with your meals.

If you have a sweet tooth or you enjoy baking a lot, consider making your own pie filling and juices using fresh ingredients. Having stocks of pie fillings allows you to make pies for yourself, your family, and even unexpected guests quickly. As for juices, there is nothing more refreshing than drinking juice made from real fruits and vegetables. It's also possible to preserve homemade condiments and dressings like ketchup, mustard, and vinaigrettes using your water bath canner.

Salsas and Sauces

Salsas and sauces are also considered high-acid foods because you will be adding components to them that are high in acid. These components make them suitable for water bath canning. Just make sure to use natural ingredients instead of artificial chemicals to ensure that the final product will always be healthy and of high quality.

Tomatoes

Technically, a tomato is a fruit even though it's often treated as a vegetable in cooking. It's possible to can whole tomatoes or use them as the main ingredient for salsa, juice, sauce, and more.

Vegetables

Some types of vegetables such as rhubarb can also be canned through this method. However, most types of vegetables need to undergo pickling or fermenting first before they can safely be processed. When it comes to veggies, you should always make sure that the recipe indicates that it is suitable for water bath canning, not pressure canning.

When it comes to adding more acid to low-acid ingredients, the key here is to find the right balance. Adding enough acid prevents the food from getting spoiled. Pay attention to the kind of acid you should add along with the quantity. This is very important, especially since water bath canning doesn't reach high enough temperatures during the canning process.

THE WORST FOODS TO PRESERVE (AND WHY)

You have already learned how low-acid foods cannot be processed through water bath canning because this method doesn't reach temperatures that are high enough to destroy botulism and other types of bacteria. Although you can process some types of low-acid foods by adding acidic components, there are certain foods that shouldn't be preserved through water bath canning because of safety issues. Let's go through these foods now.

Meat, Poultry, and Seafood

Meat, poultry, and seafood can only be safely preserved using a pressure canner. Under no circumstances should you water bath can these protein sources. These foods don't contain enough acid, which means that they need to be processed at a very high temperature before being sealed. This eliminates the risk of bacteria growth and food spoilage.

Pressure canners can reach up to 240 °F, which is high enough for both raw and cooked meat, poultry, and seafood. You can even make stews and other ready-to-eat meals using these ingredients, then preserve them through pressure canning.

Most Types of Veggies

While it's possible to preserve some types of high-acid vegetables, most types of fresh veggies can't be safely processed using a water bath. Some examples of vegetables that shouldn't be processed through water bath canning include green beans, carrots, asparagus, leafy greens, and so much more. If you really want to preserve these vegetables, you need to pickle or ferment them first in order to make them suitable for processing.

Soup

Although it would be very convenient to can soup and store it in your prepper pantry, you don't have the option to do this if you will only preserve foods through water bath canning. Just like veggies, soups usually contain ingredients that are low in acid. Once you have mastered water bath canning, you may think about moving on to pressure canning if you want to expand your stockpile even further.

Vegetable, Meat, Poultry, or Seafood Stock

In order to make stock, you would have to boil either vegetables, meat, or poultry in water for a long time along with some other ingredients to season the broth. However, the end product doesn't contain enough acid for it to be safely processed through water bath canning. This method won't heat up the contents of the jars enough to destroy all bacteria that may grow or thrive in the liquid.

Dairy Products

In general, dairy products cannot be preserved using any kind of canning method. To preserve dairy products, you need to freeze-dry them. They are also low in acid and when they reach room temperature, botulism spores can grow and thrive in these foods. Therefore, you should try to avoid using these foods in pie fillings, soups, and other recipes that you plan to process through canning.

When it comes to determining the foods that shouldn't be preserved through water bath canning, check the acid levels. If you plan to search for recipes online after trying all of the recipes here, make sure that those recipes are specifically meant for water bath canning. Do this to make sure that you can eat the food you preserve at home.

Chapter 3

HOW TO START

Water bath canning is a simple process, but that doesn't mean that you can do it however you want. To preserve your foods safely, you need to follow recipes and processing times carefully. Since you will essentially try to lengthen the shelf life of various foods in order to keep them in your pantry, safety is of the essence. To help you get started, let's go through the fundamentals of water bath canning from the equipment you need to some practical tips to get you started.

BASIC EQUIPMENT NEEDED

Although you don't need any special equipment for water bath canning, you do need to prepare a number of items to start preserving your food at home. You may already have some of these items at home. If not, you can easily find them in shops that offer various kitchenware.

Pot

First, you need a large, sturdy pot that comes with a tight-fitting lid. The pot should be deep enough to hold the jars while having space above and below. Remember that you will place a rack inside the pot so that the water will boil underneath the jars. There should also be space above the jars as they need to be completely submerged in water during the water bath canning process. You can even use a Dutch oven for this purpose if you have one that is deep enough.

Canning Jars

You also need canning jars made of glass to put your food into. Purchase jars that are specifically meant for canning as these are the ones that come with proper lids and rings. It's not recommended to simply use old pickle or mayonnaise jars even if they are made of glass. Since this is where you will store your food, it's important to invest in the right types of jars that will keep your preserved foods safe.

Canning Lids

When you buy canning jars, they should already come with proper lids. Just remember that lids should only be used once for canning. Although you can reuse the jars, you need to buy new lids each time you need to process new foods for preservation.

When purchasing new lids, make sure that they will fit the jars you have at home. This ensures that the jars will be sealed tightly and keep the contents safe. After using the lids once, you can reuse them for covering jars for short-term storage or non-food storage. If you don't plan to use them anymore, you can simply discard the used lids.

Rings

Also known as bands, the rings are supposed to screw over the top of the canning jars. They are meant to hold the lids in place while you are processing the jars and their contents. After processing and cooling down the jars, remove the rings, then check to see if the lids are sealed properly. It's important to remove the rings to prevent rust from forming on the lids. Unlike canning lids, rings can be reused, as long as they still fit securely over the lids that you buy and they don't have any kind of flaw or damage.

Canning Rack

A canning rack is a rack that you place inside the canner or stockpot. This is where you place the jars during the canning process. The rack is an important part of the whole setup as it prevents the jars from being in direct contact with the bottom of the pot. It reduces the risk of the jars breaking as it keeps the jars away from the heat of the stove underneath the pot. The rack also ensures that the jars are completely immersed in boiling water throughout the processing period.

If you will invest in a canner, it should already come with a canning rack. But if you will use a stockpot that you already have at home, you may purchase a round wire rack that fits snugly in the bottom of your pot.

Other Tools and Equipment

The items mentioned above are all of the basic items you need for your water bath canning journey. Now, let's go through some other items that aren't really required, but would make the process a lot easier:

- A canning funnel would make it easier for you to fill the jars without making a mess. This is particularly useful if you won't be using wide-mouthed jars.

- A flexible plastic or rubber spatula that you can use to release air bubbles that get into the jars before processing them in the water bath.

- A measuring stick that you can use to measure the headspace of each jar before screwing on the lid. You can also use this tool to remove air bubbles that may have entered the jars while you were filling them up.

- A bubble remover is the actual tool that you would use to remove the air bubbles from inside the jars.

- A jar lifter that you can use to take the jars out of the water bath and transfer them to the place where you will allow them to cool down. You may use a pair of tongs for this purpose, but a jar lifter is much easier and safer to use.

- Cloth kitchen towels where you will place the jars after processing. You need to allow the jars to cool down undisturbed on a flat surface before storing them.

By preparing all of these items, you will be ready to start preserving different types of food to store in your prepper pantry.

GETTING STARTED WITH WATER BATH CANNING

After preparing all of the equipment you need, you should also start preparing yourself. Once you begin the process of water bath canning, it would be better if you are already familiar with all of the steps. That way, you can follow the recipe smoothly without having to stop frequently to remind yourself of the steps you need to take. Here are some tips and steps for you.

Plan Before You Process

If you are planning to stock your prepper pantry with food that you have preserved through water bath canning, you may want to practice meal planning too. This is a simple process wherein you plan your meals—or in this case, your food stocks—beforehand. Planning is an important first step so that you can buy just the right amount of ingredients needed for preservation.

Read the Recipe Carefully Before You Start

As a beginner, you should follow water bath canning recipes to ensure the best and safest results. As part of your planning process, you should also read the recipes carefully beforehand. This allows you to prepare the ingredients you need while making you familiar with all the steps you need to take throughout the water bath canning process. Familiarize yourself with the ingredients, the processing times, and the steps.

It's important to only follow recipes that have been tried and tested specifically for water bath canning. Remember that water bath canning isn't suitable for all types of foods. So if the recipe doesn't specify that you can use a water bath canner for it, find another one. The good news is that this book contains more than enough recipes for you to start with; all you have to do is read them carefully before you start.

Sterilize the Jars, but Not the Lids

It's important to sterilize the canning jars before you pack them with food. This is a very important step as it ensures that the jars are completely clean before use. You don't need to sterilize the lids, but you do need to wash them thoroughly.

After washing the lids and sterilizing the jars, make sure that they are completely dry before filling them. Any moisture could cause the contents to get spoiled. You don't need to sterilize the rings either because they won't touch the contents of the jars. It's also important to check the rims of the jars to ensure that they are free of nicks or chips. These types of damage could cause the jars to be sealed improperly.

Fill the Pot With Enough Water

When it's time to heat up your pot, place the wire rack inside it first. Then fill the pot with water making sure that there is enough to cover the jars by at least two inches. The longer the processing time is, the more water should be added. If you aren't sure, you may want to have another pot filled with boiling water on standby while you process. That way, you can keep adding water to the canner to ensure that the water level doesn't go down while processing. You may also mix a couple of tablespoons of white vinegar in the water. Although this isn't a requirement, it will prevent the outside of the jars from getting cloudy.

Know the Basic Water Bath Canning Steps

Although preparing the ingredients to fill the jars requires different steps, the steps for the actual canning process are all the same. Here are the steps:

- Prepare all of the ingredients you need.

- Heat up the water in your canner. You may sterilize the jars here, then take them out and dry them before filling.

- When you're almost ready with the jars and the contents, bring the pot to a gentle boil.

- After filling the jars, screw on the lids, and add the rings. At this point, the jars should be hot so they don't crack due to the sudden change in temperature.

- Place the jars in the pot and bring the water back to a rolling boil. Make sure that the jars are all upright and stable.

- Once the water starts boiling, cover the pot, and start timing,

- After following the recommended processing time, turn the heat off.

- Take the lid off and leave the jars in the pot for five minutes.

- Take the jars out of the pot and place them on a flat surface covered with a cloth kitchen towel.

- Leave the jars to cool down undisturbed for about 12 to 24 hours depending on what is stated in the recipe.

- After cooling, remove the rings and check the seals.

- Wipe the jars, label them with the date, and store them in your prepper pantry.

Preparing the ingredients would take varying amounts of time. For instance, raw packing ingredients wouldn't require much time compared to hot packing ingredients. This is why you need to familiarize yourself with the recipe so that you can plan your time wisely.

Make Sure There is Enough Headspace

Headspace refers to the gap between the contents of the jar and the rim. You need to measure the headspace carefully as some foods tend to expand when you process them in the water bath. Most recipes call for ¼ or ½-inch headspace. It's important to have enough headspace so that your food will be processed properly.

Take Note of Processing Times and Altitudes

The processing time is another important factor for you to take note of. Each recipe should state the exact processing time needed to preserve the ingredients. If you find a recipe that doesn't include a specific processing time, go online and search for a similar recipe. Don't worry though, the recipes here all have processing times for you to follow.

Generally, the processing times provided in recipes are for altitudes below 1,000 feet. It's important to know your altitude too as this could change the processing times of your food. Living in a place with a higher altitude means that you would have to process the food longer. If these altitudes are specified in the recipe, follow them to ensure the best and safest results.

Take Note of the Differences Between Raw and Hot Pack Preservation

Raw pack preservation involves adding raw ingredients into jars, then pouring a hot liquid into the jars before sealing them. Hot pack preservation involves adding the raw ingredients to the canning liquid, then allowing the ingredients to simmer for a certain amount of time before placing them into the jars. If a recipe includes both preparation methods, make sure to follow the correct processing times when placing the jars in the canner.

Use New Lids Each Time You Process and Remove the Rings Before Storage

While it's possible to use canning jars over and over again for processing, you shouldn't do this for the lids. When it comes to canning, lids can only be used once. Then you can use them for other purposes, but not for canning. For the jars, if you will use them again, make sure to wash them thoroughly and sterilize them before processing.

Unlike lids, rings can be reused for canning purposes. Just wash them well first before using them again. Make sure to remove the rings before storing the jars as this is an important safety standard.

Make Sure That the Jars are Sealed Properly

After removing the rings, check the lids to make sure that the jars are sealed properly. The lids should be screwed onto the jars tightly. They shouldn't wobble when you take the rings off. If you notice any loose lids, check if the contents are still edible. If they are, consume them right away. Never store jars that have been improperly sealed.

Label and Store the Jars Properly

After making sure that the jars are properly sealed, label each of them with their processing date. This is important so that you can rotate your stocks regularly. Although foods that have been preserved through water bath canning can last for months or even years, you shouldn't wait for the expiration date to consume them.

Generally, foods canned at home last between 12 to 18 months. Over time, their quality declines in terms of texture, nutrition, and flavor. Although still safe to eat, they won't be as good as when you first processed them. For this reason, it's recommended that you schedule your canning sessions for every few months or so. That way, you can replace the old stocks with new ones and enjoy those old stocks before they get spoiled.

Make sure to store the preserved foods in a cool, dark place. If you already have a prepper pantry ready, store your jars there. If not, you can keep them in the basement, a cold storage area, or even in one of the cupboards in your pantry. The key here is to find a place where the temperature remains fairly constant to prevent early spoilage of your food items.

Wash All of Your Tools and Equipment After Use

Each time you finish a water bath canning session, you need to wash everything that you used. For best results, use hot, soapy water to clean your items, then rinse them well. After that, make sure to dry everything completely before storing them. Do this to maintain the quality of your water bath canning items so you can keep using them each time you need to preserve batches of food.

Never Make Up Your Own Canning Recipes

It can't be stated enough—follow canning recipes carefully. Remember that these recipes have been tested to ensure their safety. This is especially important if you are new to water bath canning. Avoid doing things like:

- Adding more vegetables to dilute relish or salsa recipes. Remember that vegetables are low-acid foods. Adding more than what is indicated in a recipe will mess up the balance and increase the risk of spoilage.

- Adding more starch to a recipe just to thicken it. Doing this reduces the ability of the heat to penetrate into the jars and the ingredients, thus resulting in under-processed or undercooked food.

These are just some examples of seemingly harmless recipe modifications that could result in unsafe results. Keep all of these tips in mind when it's time for you to start canning your first batch of preserves. The more you practice, the easier the process becomes. Then you will feel comfortable enough to try more complex recipes to add more variety to your stockpile.

Chapter 4

PREPARING YOUR PREPPER PANTRY

From the beginning of this book, you may have noticed the term "prepper pantry" being used quite often. This is because most people who become interested in preserving their own food at home want to start storing food for emergencies and other unexpected occurrences.

Simply put, a prepper pantry is a stockpile of various items that you store in one area or room in your home. Also known as a survival pantry, you can fill this space with preserved foods and other essential non-food items. The main purpose of having a prepper pantry is to provide what you and your family would need in case of an unexpected situation or emergency.

While you can store canned goods and other ready-made food items in your prepper pantry, making your own preserved foods is recommended if you want to have the most nutritious items in your storage space. Since you will be canning your own food at home, you won't have to worry about added chemicals or artificial ingredients that might compromise your health.

Before we dive into the different water bath canning recipes, let's focus on preparing your prepper pantry. That way, you can have it ready to store all of the delicious preserves you will process in your water bath canner.

THE BENEFITS OF HAVING A PREPPER PANTRY

You can build your prepper pantry either for short-term or long-term storage depending on your goals. If you want to have a prepper pantry for long-term food storage, adding canned foods is a good start. If you're wondering why having a prepper pantry is a good idea, here are some benefits to look forward to.

Food Security

When something bad happens like a natural disaster, a pandemic, or any other event that affects the general public, the first thing people do is flock to the local food shops to stock up on food supplies. In those situations, you would have to act quickly as all types of food will be flying off the shelves. If you have a prepper pantry at home that's filled with healthy and nutritious food, you won't have to join the other panic buyers. Instead, you can focus on keeping your family safe.

Peace of Mind

Even if nothing unexpected occurs, having a prepper pantry will give you peace of mind. Instead of worrying about potential catastrophes, you will feel confident that you can provide your family with the food they need while other people are fighting for whatever stocks are left in supermarkets. If you or any of your family members have allergies or other special dietary needs, having a prepper pantry becomes even more important as you won't have to worry about not finding the right foods to feed your family.

Convenience

This is another excellent benefit, especially if you live a very busy life. If some unexpected guests drop by your home, you will always have something to serve them. Simply take something from your stockpile, heat it up, and you're good to go! You can do the same thing if you don't have time to cook a proper meal for your family. Just make sure to replace the foods you have consumed with newly preserved foods to keep your survival pantry well-stocked.

Customization

Another great thing about having your own stockpile is that you can fill it with whatever foods you want. Just because you're preparing for emergency situations, that doesn't mean that you should settle for food that you don't like. When planning what to store in your survival pantry, make sure to include foods that you and your family like. Since you will be canning your own foods at home, you have the freedom to choose what to include and what to omit. That way, you can look forward to eating delicious foods even during emergencies or any other unexpected events.

Absolutely anyone can benefit from having a prepper pantry at home, and you don't have to break the bank to build one. Create a plan first, then start adding more foods to your stockpile over time. Before you know it, you will already have a fully stocked pantry along with all of these wonderful benefits to look forward to!

TIPS FOR PLANNING YOUR PREPPER PANTRY

Having a prepper pantry at home is a truly wonderful thing, but building one isn't a simple task. You need to plan it well to ensure that the stockpile you create serves its purpose. To make things easier for you, here are some tips to keep in mind.

Create a Plan

As with any new endeavor, creating a plan for your prepper pantry is the first step. Think about your purpose or goal, what type of pantry you want to have, the foods you want to put in the pantry, and more. Take a moment to sit down and write (or type) all of your ideas. While brainstorming, you don't have to be too strict with yourself. After you have poured out all of your ideas on paper, go back to the list you have made. Pick out the best ideas you have and organize them. With a clear plan in front of you, building your prepper pantry will be a much easier task.

Determine the Location of Your Prepper Pantry

One of the most important things to decide when building a prepper pantry is where you will place it. Since you will be storing food in this space, you need a place that's predominantly dark and cool. It should also be free of pests and moisture. If you have a lot of rooms in your home, you can simply pick one to use as the location of your stockpile. If not, you can use an area of one of your rooms instead. Even though your prepper pantry won't be as big as you want it, if you find the right location, it will be a success.

Build Your Prepper Pantry Gradually

Once you have your plan and you have decided on the location, it's time to start putting your plan into action. For this, you don't have to go all out right away. Trying to fill your prepper pantry in a day will cost you a lot of money! It's better to start gradually. Go back to your plan, specifically the items (both food and non-food) that you want to store in your pantry. Add these items little by little so that you won't feel pressured. You want this to be a fun and fulfilling experience.

For instance, you can start with a few non-food items first since those aren't perishable. Then you can start planning which preserved foods to store. Since you will be preserving your own food through water bath canning, you have the freedom to choose which foods to process first. Keep going back to your plan. Each time you successfully add something to your pantry, cross it off your list. Continue doing this until you have stocked your prepper pantry with everything that you need.

Come Up With a Budget

Creating a budget for your stockpile will take some planning too. Right now, you may already have a food budget, which you use to feed yourself and your family every week or month. When working on your food budget, try to take a small portion from that, and use it to buy ingredients for your food preservation. Since you won't completely fill up your pantry with food immediately, you won't need a big budget for this purpose.

When it's time to shop for ingredients, try to search for discounts, sales, and other deals that will help you save money. You can even buy ingredients in bulk, then use these for food preservation and for your weekly meals. Take time to compare prices from different food shops and try to get your hands on coupons whenever possible. Doing all of these things may take some effort, but it will all be worth it once you see that your prepper pantry is filling up with essential items.

Focus on Nutrition and Variety

Think about these factors when deciding the foods to store in your prepper pantry. You want to avoid canned and frozen foods that are highly processed as they typically contain artificial ingredients that aren't good for your health. So when planning what foods to store in your stockpile, think about the nutrient content. That way, you will feel good about what you and your family will eat even in difficult situations.

To make things interesting, come up with different options too. When dealing with an emergency, having to eat the same thing each day might make you feel even more stressed. Fortunately, this doesn't have to be the case. You have the freedom to choose what goes into your pantry. Fill it with different types of food so you will have something to look forward to no matter how bleak the situation gets.

Rotate Your Stocks

Preserving your own food at home allows you to create delicious and nutritious food items with longer shelf lives. However, it's important to remember that home-canned foods don't last as long as processed, store-bought ones. This is because you won't be using chemicals or artificial additives in the preservation process.

This is why it's important to label each of your food jars with the processing date. Then you need to rotate your stocks regularly. This simply means that you regularly preserve new stocks through water bath canning, then replace the old ones with the new ones. When you will do this depends on the shelf life of your existing stocks. After replacing the old stocks with new ones, you can consume the old stocks. Include them in your weekly meal plan so that you can enjoy them without wasting any food.

Try to come up with a system for rotating your stocks. For instance, when planning what foods to preserve, group them according to their shelf life. That way, you can repeat the same process after a certain number of months for the purpose of rotation. Avoid replacing too many jars at the same time as you might end up with too much food that you need to consume. Finally, don't wait until the expiration date is too close as you might not be able to eat your old stocks before they get spoiled. If you can't eat all of your old stocks, consider gifting them to your friends and loved ones so they don't go to waste.

Start Meal Planning

Meal planning is a simple process that works very well with building a prepper pantry. This process typically involves planning your meals every week. It allows you to be aware of what you have and what you need. By meal planning, you can be more efficient at planning your budget and your stock-rotation system.

When it comes to planning your prepper pantry, the key is to go at your own pace. It can take a couple of weeks, a couple of months, or even a year or so to fully stock your pantry. As the days go by, keep checking your stocks and your list until you have completed everything you need. When you reach that point, all you have to do is to rotate your stocks regularly and enjoy the fruits of your efforts.

ALL ABOUT MEAL PLANNING AND HOW TO START

Meal planning is a very simple process. It involves setting a schedule to plan your meals for a certain period of time, usually one week. After planning your menu, write down all of the ingredients you need to cook the meals you have planned. When you have your list, you should go to the supermarket to buy everything you need. After that, you can prep the ingredients at home and cook all of your meals.

When you're done, allow the meals to cool down completely before covering the containers and storing them in your refrigerator. This will provide homemade meals for the whole week. All you need to do is reheat them when the time is right.

Meal planning is highly recommended when you're starting a new diet or when you just want to start eating healthier meals. It saves time and money, and it teaches you to make healthier food choices. By meal planning, you can also keep yourself updated on the stocks you have in your prepper pantry as you can include your old stocks in your meal plans. To start meal planning, here are some practical pointers:

- As with building your prepper pantry, start slow when planning meals. Start by planning one meal per week first (the one you usually skip because you're too busy to cook), then keep adding as the weeks go by.

- Before you start planning your meals for the week, check your refrigerator. If you have any leftover meals from the previous week, include them on the first day in the meal plan you are making. Just check those meals first to make sure that they aren't spoiled yet.

- When planning your menu, focus on easy, simple, nutrient-dense meals for you and your family.

- Check your prepper pantry regularly as well. If you see that you have any stocks that need to be rotated, make sure to include them in your meal plan for the week.

- After planning your menu, write down all of the ingredients you need. If you will also have a canning session for that week, include the ingredients you need for that as well.

- Before going to the supermarket, check the stocks you have in your kitchen or pantry. You might have leftover ingredients that you can use. In such a case, you may cross out any duplicate ingredients from your shopping list.

- Invest in high-quality food containers to store your meals in. Airtight containers that are microwave-safe are the best. Find containers of just the right size. It would also be better if you can stack the containers to make it easier to store them in your refrigerator.

- Add variety to your diet by trying different recipes. You can find tons of easy, tasty, and healthy recipes online. Compile all of the recipes that you and your family like so that you can keep going back to them.

Meal planning takes some getting used to, especially if you have never done it before. But if you consistently plan your meals every week, this process will soon become part of your routine. Then you will realize how efficient and enjoyable meal planning is!

Chapter 5

RECIPES FOR CANNING FRUITS

Now that you have learned the basics of water bath canning, it's time to put that knowledge to work. There are so many foods you can preserve through water bath canning. In this chapter, you will learn how to preserve different kinds of fruits.

APRICOTS

This is a lovely recipe for fresh apricots preserved in a light syrup. The syrup will preserve the natural flavors of the apricots as it won't make them too sweet.

Time: 50 minutes

Servings: 3-quart jars

Prep Time: 20 minutes

Processing Time: 30 minutes

Ingredients:

- 2 cups of sugar

- 6 cups of water

- 9 lbs apricots (rinsed, pits removed, cut in half)

Directions:

1. Prepare the jars by heating them up in the water bath canner. Heat up the water in the canner, but not to the point of boiling.

2. In a large pot, add the sugar and water.

3. Stir well until the sugar dissolves, then bring the mixture to a boil.

4. Place the apricot halves in the jars with the cut side facing down. Make sure that there is ½-inch of headspace.

5. Pour the syrup into the jars making sure that there is ½-inch of headspace.

6. Remove the air bubbles and add more syrup as needed.

7. Wipe the rims of the jars clean, then place the seal and ring.

8. Add the jars to the water bath canner, then bring the canner to a boil.

9. Once the water is boiling, cover the water bath canner and process for 30 minutes.

10. After processing, turn off the heat and take the lid off the canner.

11. Allow to rest for about 5 minutes before taking the jars out of the hot water.

12. Place the jars on a thick kitchen towel and allow them to cool down for up to 24 hours.

13. Remove the jars, check the seals, label, and store.

BLACKBERRIES

Blackberries are a type of short-season fruit. Preserving them means that you can eat this tasty berry all year round. Use fresh blackberries for flavorful and firm results.

Time: 30 minutes

Serving Size: 2-pint jars

Prep Time: 20 minutes

Processing Time: 10 minutes

Ingredients for the syrup:

- ¼ cup of water

- 2 cups of blackberries (fresh)

Ingredients for the blackberries:

- ½ tsp nutmeg (freshly grated)

- ½ cup of brandy

- 2 cups of sugar

- 2 cups of water

- 4 cups of blackberries

- 1 cinnamon stick

Directions:

1. Prepare the jars by heating them up in the water bath canner. Heat up the water in the canner, but not to the point of boiling.

2. In a saucepan, add the blackberries over medium heat.

3. Use a fork or a potato masher to mash the blackberries slightly.

4. Add the water, stir well, and bring the mixture to a simmer.

5. Allow to simmer for about 2 minutes.

6. Use a fine-mesh strainer to strain the blackberries over a bowl. Discard the fruit pulp or use it in another recipe.

7. In a pot, add the water, sugar, nutmeg, and cinnamon stick over medium heat. Stir everything together and bring the mixture to a boil.

8. Allow to boil for about 5 minutes.

9. Add the brandy, blackberries, and the strained blackberry juice. Stir everything together and bring the mixture to a boil while stirring constantly. Be careful when stirring so you don't damage the berries.

10. Use a slotted spoon to transfer the blackberries into the heated jars making sure that there is ½-inch of headspace.

11. Pour the blackberry syrup into the jars.

12. Remove the air bubbles and add more syrup as needed.

13. Wipe the rims of the jars clean, then place the seal and ring.

14. Add the jars to the water bath canner, then bring the canner to a boil.

15. Once the water is boiling, cover the water bath canner and process for 10 minutes.

16. After processing, turn off the heat and take the lid off the canner.

17. Allow to rest for about 5 minutes before taking the jars out of the hot water.

18. Place the jars on a thick kitchen towel and allow them to cool down for up to 24 hours.

19. Remove the jars, check the seals, label, and store.

CHERRIES

If you love adding cherries to baked goods and desserts, you should try canning your own cherries at home. Canning these fresh fruits in light syrup is the best way to do this.

Time: depends on the processing time

Servings: 4-quart jars

Prep Time: 20 minutes

Processing Time: depends on the altitude

Ingredients:

- 4 ½ cups of honey

- 12 cups of water

- 10 lbs of cherries

Directions:

1. Prepare the jars by heating them up in the water bath canner. Heat up the water in the canner, but not to the point of boiling.

2. In a saucepan, add the water and honey over medium heat.

3. Stir the ingredients together until the honey dissolves completely.

4. Pour ½ cup of syrup into each of the heated jars.

5. Add the cherries to each of the jars making sure that there is ½-inch of headspace.

6. Remove the air bubbles and add more syrup as needed.

7. Wipe the rims of the jars clean, then place the seal and ring.

8. Add the jars to the water bath canner, then bring the canner to a boil.

9. Once the water is boiling, cover the water bath canner and process based on your altitude:

   a) 25 minutes for altitudes between 0 and 1,000 ft

   b) 30 minutes for altitudes between 1,001 and 3,000 ft

   c) 35 minutes for altitudes between 3,001 and 6,000 ft

   d) 40 minutes for altitudes above 6,000 ft

10. After processing, turn off the heat and take the lid off the canner.

11. Allow to rest for about 5 minutes before taking the jars out of the hot water.

12. Place the jars on a thick kitchen towel and allow them to cool down for up to 24 hours.

13. Remove the jars, check the seals, label, and store.

CRANBERRIES

Before canning whole cranberries, create a rich syrup to help preserve them. This is another seasonal fruit for you to preserve, especially if you're fond of cranberries.

Time: 35 minutes

Serving Size: 4-quart jars

Prep Time: 20 minutes

Processing Time: 15 minutes

Ingredients:

- ¾ cup of sugar

- 5 cups of water

- 12 lbs of cranberries (fresh, rinsed)

Directions:

1. Prepare the jars by heating them up in the water bath canner. Heat up the water in the canner, but not to the point of boiling.

2. In a pot, add the water and sugar over medium heat.

3. Stir the ingredients together and bring the mixture to a simmer.

4. When the mixture starts simmering, add the cranberries.

5. Allow to simmer for about 1 to 2 minutes until the berries are heated through and they are starting to crack.

6. Scoop the cranberries and the syrup into the heated canning jars making sure that there is ½-inch of headspace.

7. Remove the air bubbles and add more syrup as needed.

8. Wipe the rims of the jars clean, then place the seal and ring.

9. Add the jars to the water bath canner, then bring the canner to a boil.

10. Once the water is boiling, cover the water bath canner and process for 15 minutes.

11. After processing, turn off the heat and take the lid off the canner.

12. Allow to rest for about 5 minutes before taking the jars out of the hot water.

13. Place the jars on a thick kitchen towel and allow them to cool down for up to 24 hours.

14. Remove the jars, check the seals, label, and store.

FRUIT COCKTAIL

If you like buying fruit cocktails in supermarkets, why don't you try making your own fruity mixture at home. Here is a basic recipe but you can always switch up the fruits.

Time: 50 minutes

Serving Size: 3-quart jars

Prep Time: 30 minutes

Processing Time: 20 minutes

Ingredients:

- 3 cups of sugar

- 4 cups of water

- 1 ½ lbs green grapes (seedless, slightly under ripe)

- 3 lbs peaches (fresh)

- 3 lbs pears (fresh)

- ⅔ lbs maraschino cherries (jarred)

- Lemon juice (for soaking the fruits)

Directions:

1. Rinse the grapes, then place them in a bowl filled with lemon juice.

2. Bring a pot of water to a boil over medium heat.

3. Once the water starts boiling, add the peaches and cook for about 1 to 2 minutes.

4. Transfer the peaches to a bowl filled with cold water, then slip the skins off.

5. Slice the peaches in half, remove the pits, and cut into cubes.

6. Add the peach cubes to the bowl with the grapes.

7. Peel the pears, cut them in half, and remove the cores.

8. Cut up the pears into cubes, then add them to the bowl.

9. Prepare the jars by heating them up in the water bath canner. Heat up the water in the canner, but not to the point of boiling.

10. In a pot, add the water and sugar over medium heat. Stir the ingredients together until the sugar dissolves completely. Bring to a boil.

11. Once the syrup starts boiling, turn the heat down. Allow to boil gently.

12. Drain and discard the lemon juice from the bowl with the mixed fruits.

13. Add ½ cup of boiling syrup into each of the heated jars.

14. Divide the cherries among the jars, then add the mixed fruits making sure that there is ½-inch of headspace.

15. Remove the air bubbles and add more syrup as needed.

16. Wipe the rims of the jars clean, then place the seal and ring.

17. Add the jars to the water bath canner, then bring the canner to a boil.

18. Once the water is boiling, cover the water bath canner and process for 20 minutes.

19. After processing, turn off the heat and take the lid off the canner.

20. Allow to rest for about 5 minutes before taking the jars out of the hot water.

21. Place the jars on a thick kitchen towel and allow them to cool down for up to 24 hours.

22. Remove the jars, check the seals, label, and store.

GRAPES

Grapes that have been preserved through water bath canning maintain their texture and flavor. This is a wonderful thing to consider, especially if you're fond of grapes.

Time: depends on the processing time

Servings: 4-quart jars

Prep Time: 10 minutes

Processing Time: depends on the altitude

Ingredients:

- ¾ cups of sugar

- 5 cups of water

- 8 lbs of grapes (firm, slightly underripe)

Directions:

1. Wash the grapes and remove the stems.

2. Prepare the jars by heating them up in the water bath canner. Heat up the water in the canner, but not to the point of boiling.

3. Bring a pot of water to a boil over medium heat.

4. Once the water is boiling, add the grapes. Blanche the grapes for about 45 seconds to 1 minute.

5. Use a slotted spoon to remove the grapes and transfer them to a bowl.

6. In a saucepan, add the water and sugar over medium heat.

7. Stir the ingredients together until the sugar dissolves completely.

8. Add the grapes to the heated jars making sure that there is ½-inch of headspace.

9. Pour the hot syrup into each of the jars.

10. Remove the air bubbles and add more syrup as needed.

11. Wipe the rims of the jars clean, then place the seal and ring.

12. Add the jars to the water bath canner, then bring the canner to a boil.

13. Once the water is boiling, cover the water bath canner and process for 10 minutes. For varying altitudes, take note of the following processing times:

14. 20 minutes for altitudes between 0 and 1,000 feet

15. 25 minutes for altitudes between 1,001 and 3,000 feet

16. 30 minutes for altitudes between 3,001 and 6,000 feet

17. 35 minutes for altitudes above 6,001 feet

18. After processing, turn off the heat and take the lid off the canner.

19. Allow to rest for about 5 minutes before taking the jars out of the hot water.

20. Place the jars on a thick kitchen towel and allow them to cool down for up to 24 hours.

21. Remove the jars, check the seals, label, and store.

KIWI

When choosing kiwis for canning, opt for firm fruits instead of mushy ones. As this fruit is processed, it will gain a lighter color and a milder flavor.

Time: 50 minutes

Serving Size: 4-quart jars

Prep Time: 30 minutes

Processing Time: 20 minutes

Ingredients:

- 2 cups of sugar

- 4 cups of water

- 12 lbs kiwi

Directions:

1. Wash the kiwi fruits, peel them, and slice as desired.

2. Prepare the jars by heating them up in the water bath canner. Heat up the water in the canner, but not to the point of boiling.

3. In a pot, add the water over medium heat and bring to a simmer.

4. Once the water starts to simmer, add the sugar. Mix well until the sugar dissolves completely. Bring to a gentle boil.

5. Add the kiwi slices to the pot. Mix gently and cook for about 2 to 3 minutes.

6. Fill the jars with the kiwi slices and syrup, making sure that there is ½-inch of headspace.

7. Remove the air bubbles and add more syrup as needed.

8. Wipe the rims of the jars clean, then place the seal and ring.

9. Add the jars to the water bath canner, then bring the canner to a boil.

10. Once the water is boiling, cover the water bath canner and process for 20 minutes.

11. After processing, turn off the heat and take the lid off the canner.

12. Allow to rest for about 5 minutes before taking the jars out of the hot water.

13. Place the jars on a thick kitchen towel and allow them to cool down for up to 24 hours.

14. Remove the jars, check the seals, label, and store.

LEMONS

Although lemons are always available, it's still a good idea to can them at home. Having lemons in your prepper pantry allows you to use this fruit whenever you need it.

Time: 30 minutes

Serving Size: 3-quart jars

Prep Time: 25 minutes

Processing Time: 5 minutes

Ingredients:

- 6 cups of sugar

- 18 lemons (rinsed thoroughly)

Directions:

1. Prepare the jars by washing them thoroughly. Do the same for the lids and the rings. Sterilize everything well.

2. Use a sharp knife to slice each of the lemons into 6 slices.

3. Sprinkle sugar into one jar, then place 3 slices of lemon on top of it. Keep adding layers of sugar and lemon slices until you reach the top. The last layer should be a layer of sugar.

4. Cover the jar with a clean piece of cotton cloth, then secure the cloth using a rubber band.

5. Repeat the filling steps for the rest of the jars.

6. Place the jars in the refrigerator and leave them there overnight. By doing this, the sugar will melt and turn into syrup.

7. The next day, take the jars out. Leave them on the counter to warm up to room temperature.

8. Prepare the water bath canner by adding water to it and heating it up.

9. Open the jars and remove the cotton cloth. Wipe the rims of the jars clean, then place the seal and ring.

10. Add the jars to the water bath canner, then bring the canner to a boil.

11. Once the water is boiling, cover the water bath canner and process for 5 minutes.

12. After processing, turn off the heat and take the lid off the canner.

13. Allow to rest for about 5 minutes before taking the jars out of the hot water.

14. Place the jars on a thick kitchen towel and allow them to cool down for up to 24 hours.

15. Remove the jars, check the seals, label, and store.

MANGO

You may can mangoes at home to preserve this fruit as it can get expensive when it's not in season. Mangoes are very versatile, which means you can use them in different ways.

Time: 40 minutes

Serving Size: 3-quart jars

Prep Time: 20 minutes

Processing Time: 20 minutes

Ingredients:

- ½ cup of sugar

- ¾ cup of lemon juice (fresh)

- 4 cups of water

- 18 mangoes

Directions:

1. Prepare the jars by heating them up in the water bath canner. Heat up the water in the canner, but not to the point of boiling.

2. Slice the mangoes, scoop the flesh out, and cut the flesh into cubes.

3. Fill the jars with the mango cubes making sure that there is ½-inch of headspace.

4. Pour ¼ cup of lemon juice into each of the jars. Set the jars aside while you prepare the syrup.

5. In a pot, add the water over medium heat.

6. Mix well until the sugar dissolves completely, then bring the mixture to a boil.

7. Pour the syrup into each of the jars with mango cubes.

8. Remove the air bubbles and add more syrup as needed.

9. Wipe the rims of the jars clean, then place the seal and ring.

10. Add the jars to the water bath canner, then bring the canner to a boil.

11. Once the water is boiling, cover the water bath canner and process for 20 minutes.

12. After processing, turn off the heat and take the lid off the canner.

13. Allow to rest for about 5 minutes before taking the jars out of the hot water.

14. Place the jars on a thick kitchen towel and allow them to cool down for up to 24 hours.

15. Remove the jars, check the seals, label, and store.

PEACHES

Peaches are a versatile fruit that can be processed in a water bath canner easily. For this recipe, you will preserve the peaches in a light syrup to maintain their natural flavor.

Time: 1 hour, 20 minutes

Serving Size: 4-quart jars

Prep Time: 1 hour

Processing Time: 20 minutes

Ingredients:

- ⅛ cup of lemon juice

- ¾ cup of sugar

- 2 ¾ cups of water

- 9 lbs peaches

- Ice

Directions:

1. Prepare the jars by heating them up in the water bath canner. Heat up the water in the canner, but not to the point of boiling.

2. Fill a bowl with water and lemon juice.

3. Use a paring knife to cut the peaches in half, then remove the pits. Place the peach halves in the bowl of lemon water.

4. In a pot, add the water and sugar over medium heat. Stir well until the sugar dissolves, then bring the mixture to a boil.

5. Once the syrup is boiling, fill a bowl with water and ice.

6. Add the peach halves into the pot with the syrup and cook them for about 1 minute. If needed, cook the peach halves in batches.

7. Use a slotted spoon to transfer the peach halves to the bowl with ice water for about 1 minute.

8. Gently peel the skin off the peach halves, then place them in the heated jars with the cut side facing down.

9. Pour the syrup into each of the jars making sure that there is ½-inch of headspace.

10. Remove the air bubbles and add more syrup as needed.

11. Wipe the rims of the jars clean, then place the seal and ring.

12. Add the jars to the water bath canner, then bring the canner to a boil.

13. Once the water is boiling, cover the water bath canner and process for 20 minutes.

14. After processing, turn off the heat and take the lid off the canner.

15. Allow to rest for about 5 minutes before taking the jars out of the hot water.

16. Place the jars on a thick kitchen towel and allow them to cool down for up to 12 hours.

17. Remove the jars, check the seals, label, and store.

PEARS

When choosing pears to can, opt for firm, ripe ones. Also, choose fruits that don't have spoiled spots to ensure that you only get the highest-quality fruits in your jars.

Time: 50 minutes

Serving Size: 4-quart jars

Prep Time: 20 minutes

Processing Time: 30 minutes

Ingredients:

- ½ cup of lemon juice (fresh)

- 6 cups of water (for preserving the pears)

- 16 cups of water (for treating the pears)

- 12 lbs pears (rinsed well)

Directions:

1. Prepare the jars by heating them up in the water bath canner. Heat up the water in the canner, but not to the point of boiling.

2. In a pot, add some water and bring to a boil.

3. In a bowl, add the water and lemon juice, then mix well.

4. Cut the pears in half or quarters. Remove the seeds and any spoiled spots.

5. Add the pear halves to the bowl. Soak them for about 2 to 3 minutes.

6. Place the pear halves in the heated jars.

7. Pour boiling water into each of the jars making sure that there is ½-inch of headspace.

8. Remove the air bubbles and add more water as needed.

9. Wipe the rims of the jars clean, then place the seal and ring.

10. Add the jars to the water bath canner, then bring the canner to a boil.

11. Once the water is boiling, cover the water bath canner and process for 30 minutes.

12. After processing, turn off the heat and take the lid off the canner.

13. Allow to rest for about 5 minutes before taking the jars out of the hot water.

14. Place the jars on a thick kitchen towel and allow them to cool down for up to 12 hours.

15. Remove the jars, check the seals, label, and store.

PLUMS

Plums are a very versatile fruit that can be used in different ways. For this recipe, you will be making spiced plums for a tasty and healthy canned treat.

Time: 40 minutes

Serving Size: 5-quart jars

Prep Time: 20 minutes

Processing Time: 20 minutes

Ingredients:

- 4 cups of honey

- 10 cups of water

- 8 lbs plums (rinsed well)

- 4 oranges (juiced, zested)

- 10 cinnamon sticks

- 30 cloves

Directions:

1. Prepare the jars by heating them up in the water bath canner. Heat up the water in the canner, but not to the point of boiling.

2. In a pot, add the water, cinnamon sticks, honey, and orange juice over medium heat. Stir the ingredients well and bring the mixture to a boil.

3. Once the mixture starts boiling, turn the heat down to low. Allow to simmer for about 10 minutes while stirring frequently.

4. While the syrup simmers, cut the plums in half and remove the pits.

5. Add the plum halves to the pot, then bring the mixture back to a boil while stirring frequently.

6. Once the mixture starts boiling, turn the heat off.

7. Prepare the jars by adding 1 teaspoon of orange zest and a few cloves to each of them.

8. Use a slotted spoon to fish out the cinnamon sticks, then add 2 sticks to each jar.

9. Add the plums and syrup into each of the jars making sure that there is ½-inch of headspace.

10. Remove the air bubbles and add more water as needed.

11. Wipe the rims of the jars clean, then place the seal and ring.

12. Add the jars to the water bath canner, then bring the canner to a boil.

13. Once the water is boiling, cover the water bath canner and process for 20 minutes.

14. After processing, turn off the heat and take the lid off the canner.

15. Allow to rest for about 5 minutes before taking the jars out of the hot water.

16. Place the jars on a thick kitchen towel and allow them to cool down for up to 24 hours.

17. Remove the jars, check the seals, label, and store.

RASPBERRIES

It's very easy to preserve raspberries through water bath canning and the result is amazingly tasty. Eat the preserved fruits on their own or add them to various dishes.

Time: 25 minutes

Serving Size: 3-quart jars

Prep Time: 15 minutes

Processing Time: 10 minutes

Ingredients:

- 6 cups of sugar (granulated)

- 6 ¾ cups of water

- 9 lbs raspberries (fresh, rinsed well)

Directions:

1. Prepare the jars by heating them up in the water bath canner. Heat up the water in the canner, but not to the point of boiling.

2. In a pot, add the water and sugar over medium heat. Stir well until the sugar dissolves, then bring the mixture to a boil.

3. Once the mixture starts boiling, take the pot off the heat. Allow the syrup to cool down for about 5 minutes.

4. Add the raspberries into each of the jars making sure that there is ½-inch of headspace.

5. Pour the hot syrup into the jars.

6. Remove the air bubbles and add more syrup as needed.

7. Wipe the rims of the jars clean, then place the seal and ring.

8. Add the jars to the water bath canner, then bring the canner to a boil.

9. Once the water is boiling, cover the water bath canner and process for 10 minutes.

10. After processing, turn off the heat and take the lid off the canner.

11. Allow to rest for about 5 minutes before taking the jars out of the hot water.

12. Place the jars on a thick kitchen towel and allow them to cool down for up to 24 hours.

13. Remove the jars, check the seals, label, and store.

Chapter 6

RECIPES FOR CANNING VEGETABLES

After canning different types of fruits, it's time to start canning veggies. The challenge with canning veggies is that most of them are low in acid. Because of this, you have to pickle some types of vegetables first before preserving them in your water bath canner. In this chapter, you will learn how to can different types of raw or pickled vegetables.

CANDIED JALAPEÑOS

Candied jalapeños are wonderfully delicious with their hot and sweet flavors. Use these preserves as a versatile condiment in various dishes.

Time: 45 minutes

Serving Size: 3-quart jars

Prep Time: 20 minutes

Cook Time: 25 minutes

Ingredients:

- 1 tsp cinnamon

- 1 tsp ginger (fresh, grated)

- 1 tsp turmeric

- 1 ½ cups of white vinegar

- 3 cups of white sugar

- 3 lbs jalapeños (sliced)

Directions:

1. Prepare the jars by heating them up in the water bath canner. Heat up the water in the canner, but not to the point of boiling.

2. In a pot, add the sugar, vinegar, turmeric, cinnamon, and ginger over medium-high heat. Stir everything together and bring the mixture to a boil.

3. Once the mixture starts boiling, turn the heat down to low. Allow to simmer for about 5 to 7 minutes until it reduces into a syrup.

4. Turn the heat back up to medium-high and add the jalapeños to the pot.

5. Stir well and bring the mixture to a boil.

6. Once the mixture starts boiling, turn the heat down to low. Allow to simmer for about 5 minutes.

7. Add the jalapeños and syrup into each of the jars making sure that there is ½-inch of headspace.

8. Remove the air bubbles and add more syrup as needed.

9. Wipe the rims of the jars clean, then place the seal and ring.

10. Add the jars to the water bath canner, then bring the canner to a boil.

11. Once the water is boiling, cover the water bath canner and process for 10 minutes.

12. After processing, turn off the heat and take the lid off the canner.

13. Allow to rest for about 5 minutes before taking the jars out of the hot water.

14. Place the jars on a thick kitchen towel and allow them to cool down for up to 24 hours.

15. Remove the jars, check the seals, label, and store.

DILL PICKLES

Here is an easy canning recipe for you to make your own dill pickles. The pickles you will preserve will be crunchy, tasty, and perfectly tangy.

Time: 45 minutes

Serving Size: 3-quart jars

Prep Time: 30 minutes

Cook Time: 15 minutes

Ingredients:

- ¼ tsp peppercorns (whole)

- ½ tsp mustard seeds

- 4 tbsp + 2 tsp salt

- ½ cup of cane sugar (preferably organic)

- 2 ½ cups + 1 tbsp water

- 2 ½ cups + 1 tbsp white vinegar

- 4 lbs pickling cucumbers (rinsed well)

- 1 bay leaf

- 2 allspice berries

- 2 cloves (whole)

- 6 sprigs of dill (fresh)

Directions:

1. Prepare the jars by heating them up in the water bath canner. Heat up the water in the canner, but not to the point of boiling.

2. In a saucepan, add the vinegar, water, salt, and sugar over medium heat.

3. Add the mustard seeds, peppercorns, bay leaf, cloves, and allspice berries to a cheesecloth, then wrap them up to make a spice bag.

4. Add the spice bag to the saucepan. Stir everything together, then bring the mixture to a boil.

5. Once the mixture starts boiling, turn the heat down to low. Allow to simmer for about 15 minutes while stirring occasionally.

6. Slice the cucumbers and add them into each of the jars making sure that there is ½-inch of headspace.

7. Add 2 sprigs of dill into each of the jars too.

8. Pour the hot brine into the jars.

9. Remove the air bubbles and add more brine as needed.

10. Wipe the rims of the jars clean, then place the seal and ring.

11. Add the jars to the water bath canner, then bring the canner to a boil.

12. Once the water is boiling, cover the water bath canner and process for 15 minutes.

13. After processing, turn off the heat and take the lid off the canner.

14. Allow to rest for about 5 minutes before taking the jars out of the hot water.

15. Place the jars on a thick kitchen towel and allow them to cool down for up to 24 hours.

16. Remove the jars, check the seals, label, and store.

MUSHROOMS

For this recipe, you will marinate the mushrooms first before preserving them. This helps with the preservation process so that you can use the water bath canning method.

Time: 40 minutes

Serving Size: 4-quart jars

Prep Time: 20 minutes

Cook Time: 20 minutes

Ingredients:

- 1 tbsp basil (dried)

- 1 tbsp oregano (dried)

- 1 tbsp pickling salt

- ¼ cup of pimento (diced)

- ½ cup of lemon juice (bottled)

- ½ cup of onions (finely chopped)

- 2 cups of olive oil

- 3 cups of white vinegar (preferably with 5% acidity)

- 7 lbs mushrooms (whole, rinsed well, half of the stems cut off)

- 2 cloves of garlic (cut in quarters)

- 25 black peppercorns (whole)

- Water (for cooking the mushrooms)

Directions:

1. In a pot, add the water, lemon juice, and mushrooms over medium heat. Stir everything well, then bring the mixture to a boil.

2. Once the mixture starts boiling, turn the heat down to low. Cover the pot with a lid and allow to simmer for about 5 minutes.

3. Drain and discard the liquid from the pot. Cover the pot and set aside.

4. Prepare the jars by heating them up in the water bath canner. Heat up the water in the canner, but not to the point of boiling.

5. In another pot, add the vinegar, olive oil, basil, oregano, salt, pimiento, and onion over medium heat. Stir everything well, then bring the mixture to a boil.

6. Once the mixture starts boiling, take the pot off the heat.

7. Divide the garlic and peppercorns between the jars.

8. Fill each of the jars with mushrooms making sure that there is ½-inch of headspace.

9. Pour the marinade into the jars and mix well.

10. Remove the air bubbles and add more marinade as needed.

11. Wipe the rims of the jars clean, then place the seal and ring.

12. Add the jars to the water bath canner, then bring the canner to a boil.

13. Once the water is boiling, cover the water bath canner and process for 20 minutes.

14. After processing, turn off the heat and take the lid off the canner.

15. Allow to rest for about 5 minutes before taking the jars out of the hot water.

16. Place the jars on a thick kitchen towel and allow them to cool down for up to 24 hours.

17. Remove the jars, check the seals, label, and store.

PICKLED ASPARAGUS

You need to pickle asparagus first before preserving it through water bath canning. After pickling, this becomes a shelf-stable veggie that deserves a place in your prepper pantry.

Time: 25 minutes

Serving Size: 3-quart jars

Prep Time: 15 minutes

Cook Time: 10 minutes

Ingredients for the asparagus:

- 10 ½ lbs asparagus spears (fresh, ends trimmed)

- A handful of dill weed (fresh)

Ingredients for the pickling brine:

- 3 tsp allspice berries

- 6 tsp mustard seeds

- 6 tsp coriander seeds

- 3 tbsp dill seeds

- 6 tbsp cane sugar

- ¾ cup of pickling salt

- 7 ½ cups of water

- 7 ½ cups of white vinegar (preferably with 5% acidity)

- 12 cloves of garlic (minced)

Directions:

1. Prepare the jars by heating them up in the water bath canner. Heat up the water in the canner, but not to the point of boiling.

2. Trim the ends of the asparagus spears to match the height of your canning jars making sure that there is ¼-inch headspace from the top.

3. Pack the asparagus spears into each of the heated canning jars. Also, add some sprigs of fresh dill weed between the asparagus spears.

4. In a saucepan, add all of the brine ingredients over medium heat. Stir everything together and bring the mixture to a boil.

5. Keep boiling for about 3 minutes.

6. Pour the brine into each of the jars making sure to include the solid components as well.

7. Remove the air bubbles and add more brine as needed.

8. Wipe the rims of the jars clean, then place the seal and ring.

9. Add the jars to the water bath canner, then bring the canner to a boil.

10. Once the water is boiling, cover the water bath canner and process for 10 minutes.

11. After processing, turn off the heat and take the lid off the canner.

12. Allow to rest for about 5 minutes before taking the jars out of the hot water.

13. Place the jars on a thick kitchen towel and allow them to cool down for up to 24 hours.

14. Remove the jars, check the seals, label, and store.

PICKLED BEETS

Here is an old-fashioned recipe for you to pickle beets, then preserve them through water bath canning. If you love beets, you'll surely enjoy the results.

Time: 55 minutes

Serving Size: 4-quart jars

Prep Time: 30 minutes

Cook Time: 25 minutes

Ingredients:

- 4 tsp canning salt

- 6 cups of granulated sugar

- 6 cups of white vinegar

- 10 lbs beets (rinsed well, leaves removed)

- Water (for cooking the beets)

Directions:

1. In a pot, add the water and the beets over medium heat, then bring to a boil.

2. Once the mixture starts boiling, cook the beets for about 15 minutes or until fork-tender. The actual cooking time will depend on the size of the beets

3. When the beets are tender enough, transfer them to a bowl with cold water to stop the cooking process.

4. Once the beets have cooled down, peel off the skins, and slice them thinly.

5. Prepare the jars by heating them up in the water bath canner. Heat up the water in the canner, but not to the point of boiling.

6. In another pot, add the vinegar and sugar over medium heat. Stir until the sugar dissolves, then bring the mixture to a boil.

7. Once the mixture starts boiling, take the pot off the heat.

8. Fill each of the jars with 1 teaspoon of canning salt and the sliced beets making sure that there is ½-inch of headspace.

9. Pour the brine into the jars and mix well.

10. Remove the air bubbles and add more brine as needed.

11. Wipe the rims of the jars clean, then place the seal and ring.

12. Add the jars to the water bath canner, then bring the canner to a boil.

13. Once the water is boiling, cover the water bath canner and process for 10 minutes.

14. After processing, turn off the heat and take the lid off the canner.

15. Allow to rest for about 5 minutes before taking the jars out of the hot water.

16. Place the jars on a thick kitchen towel and allow them to cool down for up to 24 hours.

17. Remove the jars, check the seals, label, and store.

PICKLED CARROTS

Pickling carrots is an easy task. You can either grow your own carrots or buy them from the supermarket, then preserve them by following this delicious recipe.

Time: 40 minutes

Serving Size: 3-quart jars

Prep Time: 20 minutes

Cook Time: 20 minutes

Ingredients for the brine:

- ½ cup of pickling salt

- 4 cups of water

- 4 cups of white vinegar

Ingredients for the carrots:

- 1 tbsp dill seed

- 6 lbs baby carrots (scrubbed)

- 6 cloves of garlic (peeled, sliced in half lengthwise)

- 6 heads of flowering dill (fresh)

Directions:

1. Prepare the jars by heating them up in the water bath canner. Heat up the water in the canner, but not to the point of boiling.

2. In a pot, add all of the brine ingredients over medium heat. Stir until the salt dissolves, then bring the mixture to a boil.

3. Once the mixture starts boiling, take the pot off the heat.

4. Fill each of the jars with garlic, dill, and baby carrots making sure that there is ½-inch of headspace.

5. Sprinkle dill seeds into each of the jars.

6. Pour the brine into the jars.

7. Remove the air bubbles and add more brine as needed.

8. Wipe the rims of the jars clean, then place the seal and ring.

9. Add the jars to the water bath canner, then bring the canner to a boil.

10. Once the water is boiling, cover the water bath canner and process for 20 minutes for altitudes up to 2,999 feet. Process for 20 minutes for altitudes above 3,000 feet.

11. After processing, turn off the heat and take the lid off the canner.

12. Allow to rest for about 5 minutes before taking the jars out of the hot water.

13. Place the jars on a thick kitchen towel and allow them to cool down for up to 24 hours.

14. Remove the jars, check the seals, label, and store.

PICKLED EGGPLANTS

Have you ever tried pickled eggplants before? This preserved veggie pairs perfectly with meat, olives, cheese, and other finger foods. They go well with sandwiches too.

Time: depends on the altitude

Serving Size: 3-quart jars

Prep Time: 20 minutes

Cook Time: depends on the altitude

Ingredients:

- ⅓ cup of kosher salt

- 3 ½ cups of water

- 3 ½ cups of white vinegar

- 5 lbs eggplants (stems removed, sliced or cut into cubes)

- 6 bay leaves

- 6 cloves of garlic (minced)

- 6 heads of dill (chopped)

Directions:

1. Prepare the jars by heating them up in the water bath canner. Heat up the water in the canner, but not to the point of boiling.

2. In a pot, add the water and vinegar over medium heat, then bring to a boil.

3. Once the mixture starts boiling, take the pot off the heat.

4. Divide the garlic cloves, dill heads, and bay leaves among the jars.

5. Fill each of the jars with the eggplant slices too.

6. Pour the brine into the jars making sure that there is ¼-inch of headspace.

7. Remove the air bubbles and add more brine as needed.

8. Wipe the rims of the jars clean, then place the seal and ring.

9. Add the jars to the water bath canner, then bring the canner to a boil.

10. Once the water is boiling, cover the water bath canner and process for 15 minutes for altitudes below 1,000 feet. For varying altitudes, take note of the following processing times:

    a) 20 minutes for altitudes between 1,001 and 3,000 feet

    b) 25 minutes for altitudes between 3,001 and 6,000 feet

    c) 30 minutes for altitudes above 6,001 feet

11. After processing, turn off the heat and take the lid off the canner.

12. Allow to rest for about 5 minutes before taking the jars out of the hot water.

13. Place the jars on a thick kitchen towel and allow them to cool down for up to 12 hours.

14. Remove the jars, check the seals, label, and store.

PICKLED GREEN BEANS

These pickled green beans are wonderfully crunchy and flavorful. They deserve a place in your prepper pantry because they are very versatile as well.

Time: 50 minutes

Serving Size: 4-quart jars

Prep Time: 10 minutes

Cook Time: 40 minutes

Ingredients:

- 2 tsp cayenne pepper
- ½ cup of salt
- 5 cups of water
- 5 cups of white vinegar
- 4 lbs green beans (fresh)
- 8 cloves of garlic
- 8 sprigs of dill (fresh)

Directions:

1. Prepare the jars by heating them up in the water bath canner. Heat up the water in the canner, but not to the point of boiling.

2. Trim the green beans so that they can fit into your canning jars.

3. In a pot, add the water, salt, and white vinegar over medium heat. Stir well and bring the mixture to a boil.

4. Once the mixture starts to boil, prepare the jars.

5. In each jar, add 2 cloves of garlic, 2 sprigs of fresh dill, and ½ teaspoon of cayenne pepper.

6. Fill each of the jars with the green beans making sure that there is ½-inch of headspace.

7. Pour the brine into the jars.

8. Remove the air bubbles and add more brine as needed.

9. Wipe the rims of the jars clean, then place the seal and ring.

10. Add the jars to the water bath canner, then bring the canner to a boil.

11. Once the water is boiling, cover the water bath canner and process for 40 minutes.

12. After processing, turn off the heat and take the lid off the canner.

13. Allow to rest for about 5 minutes before taking the jars out of the hot water.

14. Place the jars on a thick kitchen towel and allow them to cool down for up to 24 hours.

15. Remove the jars, check the seals, label, and store.

PICKLED MIXED VEGGIES

If you liked the recipe for fruit cocktail, you might enjoy this recipe too. Here, you will mix different veggies and pickle them in a garlicky brine.

Time: 40 minutes

Serving Size: 3-quart jars

Prep Time: 30 minutes

Cook Time: 10 minutes

Ingredients:

- 1 ½ tsp red pepper flakes

- 1 tbsp kosher salt

- 1 cup of sugar

- 3 cups of water

- 3 cups of white vinegar

- ¾ lb green beans (trimmed)

- **1 ⅓ lbs cauliflower florets**

- 2 ears of corn (husks removed, rinsed well, sliced)

- 2 onions (sliced into wedges)

- 3 red sweet peppers (seeded, sliced)

- 3 carrots (peeled, sliced)

- 18 cloves of garlic (smashed)

- Water (for cooking the vegetables)

Directions:

1. In a pot, add water with the cauliflower, corn, green beans, carrots, onions, and peppers over medium heat. Stir well and bring the mixture to a boil.

2. Once the mixture starts to boil, cook for about 3 minutes.

3. Drain and discard the water.

4. Prepare the jars by heating them up in the water bath canner. Heat up the water in the canner, but not to the point of boiling.

5. In another pot, add the water, sugar, salt, and vinegar over medium heat. Stir well until the sugar and salt dissolve, then bring the mixture to a boil.

6. In each jar, add 6 cloves of garlic, ½ teaspoon of red pepper flakes, and the cooked vegetables making sure that there is ½-inch of headspace.

7. Pour the brine into the jars.

8. Remove the air bubbles and add more brine as needed.

9. Wipe the rims of the jars clean, then place the seal and ring.

10. Add the jars to the water bath canner, then bring the canner to a boil.

11. Once the water is boiling, cover the water bath canner and process for 10 minutes.

12. After processing, turn off the heat and take the lid off the canner.

13. Allow to rest for about 5 minutes before taking the jars out of the hot water.

14. Place the jars on a thick kitchen towel and allow them to cool down for up to 24 hours.

15. Remove the jars, check the seals, label, and store.

PICKLED ONIONS

If you grow your own onions and you have a bountiful harvest, pickling them is a great option. This allows you to preserve your harvest and store it in your prepper pantry.

Time: 30 minutes

Serving Size: 4-quart jars

Prep Time: 20 minutes

Cook Time: 10 minutes

Ingredients:

- 2 cups of apple cider vinegar

- 2 cups of white vinegar

- 3 lbs onions (rinsed well)

- 1 clove of garlic (peeled, crushed)

Directions:

1. Prepare the jars by heating them up in the water bath canner. Heat up the water in the canner, but not to the point of boiling.

2. Peel the onions, then rinse them again.

3. Slice the onions into rings or wedges.

4. In a pot, add the garlic clove, apple cider vinegar, and white vinegar over medium heat. Stir well, then bring the mixture to a boil.

5. Once the mixture starts to boil, turn the heat down to low. Allow to simmer for about 5 minutes.

6. Add the onion slices to the jars making sure that there is ½-inch of headspace.

7. Pour the vinegar mixture into the jars.

8. Remove the air bubbles and add more vinegar as needed.

9. Wipe the rims of the jars clean, then place the seal and ring.

10. Add the jars to the water bath canner, then bring the canner to a boil.

11. Once the water is boiling, cover the water bath canner and process for 10 minutes.

12. After processing, turn off the heat and take the lid off the canner.

13. Allow to rest for about 5 minutes before taking the jars out of the hot water.

14. Place the jars on a thick kitchen towel and allow them to cool down for up to 24 hours.

15. Remove the jars, check the seals, label, and store.

SPICY PICKLED GARLIC

To process low-acid veggies in a water bath canner safely, you need to pickle them first. Here is a recipe for you to do this with garlic.

Time: depends on the processing time

Serving Size: 3-quart jars

Prep Time: 20 minutes

Cook Time: depends on the processing time

Ingredients:

- ¾ tsp red pepper flakes

- ¾ tsp thyme (dried)

- 1 ½ tsp canning salt

- 3 tsp chili powder

- 3 ½ lbs garlic cloves (peeled)

- 6 cups of white vinegar (preferably with 5% acidity)

- 1 ½ cup of cane sugar

Directions:

1. Prepare the jars by heating them up in the water bath canner. Heat up the water in the canner, but not to the point of boiling.

2. In a saucepan, add the vinegar, water, salt, thyme, chili powder, and red pepper flakes over medium-high heat.

3. Stir everything together, then bring the mixture to a boil. Allow to boil while you prepare the jars.

4. Add the garlic cloves into each of the jars making sure that there is ½-inch of headspace.

5. Pour the hot brine into the jars.

6. Remove the air bubbles and add more brine as needed.

7. Wipe the rims of the jars clean, then place the seal and ring.

8. Add the jars to the water bath canner, then bring the canner to a boil.

9. Once the water is boiling, cover the water bath canner and process for 10 minutes for altitudes of 1,000 feet and below. For varying altitudes, take note of the following processing times:

   a) 15 minutes for altitudes between 1,001 and 6,000 feet

   b) 20 minutes for altitudes above 6,001 feet

10. After processing, turn off the heat and take the lid off the canner.

11. Allow to rest for about 5 minutes before taking the jars out of the hot water.

12. Place the jars on a thick kitchen towel and allow them to cool down for up to 24 hours.

13. Remove the jars, check the seals, label, and store.

TOMATOES

Canning whole tomatoes is a good idea if you like using tomatoes when cooking. That way, you can still enjoy tomatoes even during the winter months.

Time: 1 hour, 40 minutes

Serving Size: 4-quart jars

Prep Time: 15 minutes

Cook Time: 1 hour, 25 minutes

Ingredients:

- 8 tbsp lemon juice (concentrated)

- 13 lbs tomatoes (preferably Roma tomatoes, rinsed well)

- Water (for blanching the tomatoes)

- Water (cold, for blanching the tomatoes)

Directions:

1. Use a sharp knife to score the tomatoes.

2. In a pot, add water, and bring to a boil over medium heat.

3. Once the water starts boiling, add the tomatoes. Blanche them for about 1 minute.

4. Use a slotted spoon to take out the tomatoes, and transfer them to a bowl filled with cold water.

5. Prepare the jars by heating them up in the water bath canner. Heat up the water in the canner, but not to the point of boiling.

6. When the tomatoes are cool enough to handle, peel the skins off the tomatoes.

7. Add the peeled tomatoes (and their juices) to a bowl.

8. Add 2 tablespoons of concentrated lemon juice into each of the jars.

9. Fill the jars with the tomatoes and the tomato liquid making sure that there is ½-inch of headspace.

10. Remove the air bubbles and add water as needed.

11. Wipe the rims of the jars clean, then place the seal and ring.

12. Add the jars to the water bath canner, then bring the canner to a boil.

13. Once the water is boiling, cover the water bath canner and process for 1 hour and 25 minutes.

14. After processing, turn off the heat and take the lid off the canner.

15. Allow to rest for about 5 minutes before taking the jars out of the hot water.

16. Place the jars on a thick kitchen towel and allow them to cool down for up to 24 hours.

17. Remove the jars, check the seals, label, and store.

Chapter 7

RECIPES FOR CANNING JAMS AND JELLIES

Jams and jellies are the best types of food to preserve through water bath canning, and there are so many options for you to choose from! This chapter features easy jam and jelly recipes you can start with as you learn how to master the process of water bath canning.

3-BERRY JAM

This lovely recipe combines different types of berries. That way, you can enjoy the taste of these berries all year long!

Time: 20 minutes

Serving Size: 4-pint jars

Prep Time: 10 minutes

Processing Time: 10 minutes

Ingredients:

- 4 tbsp pectin (powdered)

- ¼ cup of lemon juice (bottled)

- 3 cups of blackberries

- 3 cups of blueberries

- 3 cups of raspberries

- 10 cups of sugar (granulated)

Directions:

1. Prepare the jars by heating them up in the water bath canner. Heat up the water in the canner, but not to the point of boiling.

2. In a pot, add the blackberries, blueberries, raspberries, and lemon juice over medium heat.

3. Stir everything together and use a potato masher to mash the berries slightly.

4. Add the pectin powder and mix well.

5. Bring the berry mixture to a rolling boil while stirring constantly.

6. Once the mixture starts boiling, add the sugar.

7. Mix well and return the mixture to a boil. Continue boiling for about 1 minute while stirring constantly.

8. Take the pot off the heat and use a spoon to remove any foam on the top.

9. Use a ladle and a funnel to spoon the jam into the jars making sure that there is ¼-inch of headspace.

10. Remove the air bubbles and add more jam as needed.

11. Wipe the rims of the jars clean, then place the seal and ring.

12. Add the jars to the water bath canner, then bring the canner to a boil.

13. Once the water is boiling, cover the water bath canner and process for 10 minutes.

14. After processing, turn off the heat and take the lid off the canner.

15. Allow to rest for about 5 minutes before taking the jars out of the hot water.

16. Place the jars on a thick kitchen towel and allow them to cool down for up to 24 hours.

17. Remove the jars, check the seals, label, and store.

COCONUT AND PINEAPPLE JAM

This tasty and refreshing jam is very easy to make. The wonderful combination of ingredients will keep you wanting more.

Time: 30 minutes

Serving Size: 4-pint jars

Prep Time: 20 minutes

Processing Time: 10 minutes

Ingredients:

- 6 tbsp fruit pectin

- ½ cup of coconut (shredded, sweetened)

- ⅔ cup of coconut water (you can also use coconut rum)

- 4 ⅔ cups of pineapple (crushed)

- 6 ⅔ cups of white sugar (granulated)

Directions:

1. Prepare the jars by heating them up in the water bath canner. Heat up the water in the canner, but not to the point of boiling.

2. In a pot, add the pineapples over medium heat.

3. Use a potato masher to mash the pineapples slightly, then bring to a boil.

4. Add the pectin powder and mix well.

5. Bring the mixture to a boil while stirring constantly.

6. Once the mixture starts boiling, add the sugar, coconut, and coconut water.

7. Mix well until the sugar dissolves completely, then return the mixture to a boil while stirring constantly.

8. Turn the heat down while you fill the jars.

9. Use a ladle and a funnel to spoon the jam into the jars making sure that there is ¼-inch of headspace.

10. Remove the air bubbles and add more jam as needed.

11. Wipe the rims of the jars clean, then place the seal and ring.

12. Add the jars to the water bath canner, then bring the canner to a boil.

13. Once the water is boiling, cover the water bath canner and process for 10 minutes.

14. After processing, turn off the heat and take the lid off the canner.

15. Allow to rest for about 5 minutes before taking the jars out of the hot water.

16. Place the jars on a thick kitchen towel and allow them to cool down for up to 24 hours.

17. Remove the jars, check the seals, label, and store.

ORANGE AND FIG JAM

Combining the fresh figs with citrus flavors creates a delicious jam that you can use on desserts, bread, and more. This jam is easy to make and you don't need pectin for it.

Time: 50 minutes (sitting time not included)

Serving Size: 5-pint jars

Prep Time: 40 minutes

Processing Time: 10 minutes

Ingredients:

- 1 tbsp lemon zest

- 3 tbsp orange zest

- ½ cup of Grand Marnier

- 2 cups of sugar

- 4 ½ cups of figs (fresh, stems removed, sliced into ½-inch pieces)

- A pinch of salt

Directions:

1. In a pot, add the lemon zest, orange zest, figs, salt, and Grand Marnier.

2. Mix all of the ingredients together well.

3. Allow to sit for about 1 hour while stirring occasionally.

4. After 1 hour, place the pot over medium heat.

5. Add the sugar, mix well until the sugar dissolves completely, then bring the mixture to a boil.

6. Turn the heat down to low and allow to boil for about 30 minutes. Use a potato masher to mash the figs.

7. After about 15 minutes, prepare the jars by heating them up in the water bath canner. Heat up the water in the canner, but not to the point of boiling.

8. After boiling the jam, take the pot off the heat.

9. Use a ladle and a funnel to spoon the jam into the jars making sure that there is ¼-inch of headspace.

10. Remove the air bubbles and add more jam as needed.

11. Wipe the rims of the jars clean, then place the seal and ring.

12. Add the jars to the water bath canner, then bring the canner to a boil.

13. Once the water is boiling, cover the water bath canner and process for 10 minutes.

14. After processing, turn off the heat and take the lid off the canner.

15. Allow to rest for about 5 minutes before taking the jars out of the hot water.

16. Place the jars on a thick kitchen towel and allow them to cool down for up to 24 hours.

17. Remove the jars, check the seals, label, and store.

SALTED CANTALOUPE JAM

A lot of people wouldn't even think of making jam out of cantaloupes. But one taste of this mouthwatering jam and it might be one of your favorites!

Time: 40 minutes

Serving Size: 4-pint jars

Prep Time: 30 minutes

Processing Time: 10 minutes

Ingredients:

- 1 tsp vanilla extract

- 1 ½ tsp salt

- 2 tbsp lemon juice (freshly squeezed)

- 5 tbsp pectin (powdered)

- 4 cups of sugar (granulated, divided)

- 6 cups of cantaloupe (very ripe, peeled, diced)

Directions:

1. Prepare the jars by heating them up in the water bath canner. Heat up the water in the canner, but not to the point of boiling.

2. In a pot, add the lemon juice, cantaloupe, and 3 ½ cups of sugar over medium heat.

3. Stir all of the ingredients together and bring the mixture to a rolling boil.

4. Once the mixture starts boiling, add the pectin and the rest of the sugar. Whisk until well combined, then bring back to a rolling boil.

5. Allow to boil for about 2 to 3 minutes until it thickens to the right consistency.

6. Take the pot off the heat.

7. Add the salt and vanilla extract, then mix well.

8. Use a ladle and a funnel to spoon the jam into the jars making sure that there is ½-inch of headspace.

9. Remove the air bubbles and add more jam as needed.

10. Wipe the rims of the jars clean, then place the seal and ring.

11. Add the jars to the water bath canner, then bring the canner to a boil.

12. Once the water is boiling, cover the water bath canner and process for 10 minutes.

13. After processing, turn off the heat and take the lid off the canner.

14. Allow to rest for about 5 minutes before taking the jars out of the hot water.

15. Place the jars on a thick kitchen towel and allow them to cool down for up to 24 hours.

16. Remove the jars, check the seals, label, and store.

ZUCCHINI JAM

This zucchini jam has subtle ginger and lemon flavors making it the perfect spread with warm pastries like scones. Make sure to use fresh zucchinis for this recipe!

Time: 1 hour

Serving Size: 4-pint jars

Prep Time: 50 minutes

Processing Time: 10 minutes

Ingredients:

- 4 cups of sugar

- 2 cups of water

- 4 cups of zucchini (shredded)

- 1 4-inch piece of ginger (fresh, peeled, minced)

- 4 lemons

Directions:

1. Use a grater to zest the lemons.

2. Cut the lemons in half and squeeze the juices out.

3. Remove the seeds from the juice and set aside.

4. Chop the white pith of the lemons roughly.

5. In a pot, add the lemon seeds, chopped pith, and water over medium heat. Stir the ingredients together and bring the mixture to a boil.

6. Once the mixture starts to boil, turn the heat down to low. Allow to simmer for about 30 minutes until you get about ½ cup of thick gel.

7. Use a slotted spoon to remove the seeds and pith from the pot.

8. Prepare the jars by heating them up in the water bath canner. Heat up the water in the canner, but not to the point of boiling.

9. In the pot with the thick gel, add the lemon juice, lemon zest, zucchini, ginger, and sugar.

10. Stir all of the ingredients together and bring the mixture to a rolling boil.

11. Allow to boil for about 10 minutes until you are satisfied with the consistency.

12. Use a ladle and a funnel to spoon the jam into the jars making sure that there is ¼-inch of headspace.

13. Remove the air bubbles and add more jam as needed.

14. Wipe the rims of the jars clean, then place the seal and ring.

15. Add the jars to the water bath canner, then bring the canner to a boil.

16. Once the water is boiling, cover the water bath canner and process for 10 minutes.

17. After processing, turn off the heat and take the lid off the canner.

18. Allow to rest for about 5 minutes before taking the jars out of the hot water.

19. Place the jars on a thick kitchen towel and allow them to cool down for up to 24 hours.

20. Remove the jars, check the seals, label, and store.

CORN COB JELLY

If you have a lot of leftover corn cobs, make some jelly out of them. Here is a recipe for a sweet, spreadable jelly with a wonderful flavor.

Time: depends on the altitude

Serving Size: 4-pint jars

Prep Time: 50 minutes

Cook Time: depends on the altitude

Ingredients:

- ½ cup of fruit pectin

- 6 cups of sugar

- 16 cups of water

- 24 corn cobs (fresh, chopped into 4-inch pieces)

Directions:

1. In a saucepan, add the water and corn cobs over medium heat. Stir the ingredients together and bring the mixture to a boil.

2. Once the mixture starts boiling, turn the heat down to low. Simmer for about 35 to 40 minutes.

3. Place a fine-mesh sieve on top of a bowl, then cover it with 2 sheets of cheesecloth.

4. Pour the corn cob mixture into the sieve. Allow the liquid to drip into the bowl naturally without squeezing or pressing.

5. Prepare the jars by heating them up in the water bath canner. Heat up the water in the canner, but not to the point of boiling.

6. Pour the corn cob juice into a pot over medium heat.

7. Add the pectin powder and mix well.

8. Bring the mixture to a boil while stirring constantly. Allow to boil for about 1 minute.

9. Add the sugar and mix well until the sugar dissolves completely. Return the mixture to a boil. Allow to boil for about 5 minutes.

10. Take the pot off the heat and use a spoon to remove any foam on the top.

11. Use a ladle to pour the jelly into the jars making sure that there is ¼-inch of headspace.

12. Remove the air bubbles and add more jelly as needed.

13. Wipe the rims of the jars clean, then place the seal and ring.

14. Add the jars to the water bath canner, then bring the canner to a boil.

15. Once the water is boiling, cover the water bath canner and process for 5 minutes for altitudes of 1,000 feet and below. For varying altitudes, take note of the following processing times:

    a) 10 minutes for altitudes between 1,001 and 6,000 feet

    b) 15 minutes for altitudes above 6,001 feet

16. After processing, turn off the heat and take the lid off the canner.

17. Allow to rest for about 5 minutes before taking the jars out of the hot water.

18. Place the jars on a thick kitchen towel and allow them to cool down for up to 24 hours.

19. Remove the jars, check the seals, label, and store.

DANDELION JELLY

Have you ever tried eating dandelions? This is a unique recipe that uses the lovely flower to make a jelly that will brighten up your bread and pastries.

Time: 40 minutes (steeping time not included)

Serving Size: 3-pint jars

Prep Time: 30 minutes

Processing Time: 10 minutes

Ingredients:

- 2 tbsp lemon juice (freshly squeezed)

- 4 tbsp fruit pectin

- 4 cups of dandelion petals (rinsed, you can also use 2 cups of packed dandelion petals)

- 4 cups of sugar

- 4 cups of water

Directions:

1. In a pot, add 4 cups of water over medium heat and bring to a boil.

2. Take the pot off the heat and add the dandelion petals. Allow the petals to steep for a minimum of 1 hour up to 24 hours.

3. After steeping the petals, pour them into a fine mesh strainer placed over a bowl.

4. Squeeze and press the petals to get all of the dandelion liquid.

5. Prepare the jars by heating them up in the water bath canner. Heat up the water in the canner, but not to the point of boiling.

6. In a pot, add the dandelion tea, pectin, and lemon juice over high heat. Stir everything together and bring the mixture to a rolling boil.

7. Add the sugar and mix well until the sugar dissolves. Return the mixture to a rolling boil.

8. Allow to boil for about 1 to 2 minutes, then take the pot off the heat.

9. Use a ladle and a funnel to spoon the jelly into the jars making sure that there is ¼-inch of headspace.

10. Remove the air bubbles and add more jelly as needed.

11. Wipe the rims of the jars clean, then place the seal and ring.

12. Add the jars to the water bath canner, then bring the canner to a boil.

13. Once the water is boiling, cover the water bath canner and process for 10 minutes.

14. After processing, turn off the heat and take the lid off the canner.

15. Allow to rest for about 5 minutes before taking the jars out of the hot water.

16. Place the jars on a thick kitchen towel and allow them to cool down for up to 24 hours.

17. Remove the jars, check the seals, label, and store.

MINT JELLY

Mint jelly goes well with bread and you can even use it to brighten up lamb chops. Here's another simple recipe for you to try.

Time: depends on the processing time

Serving Size: 4-pint jars

Prep Time: 20 minutes

Processing Time: depends on the processing time

Ingredients:

- 4 tbsp pectin (powdered)

- ¼ cup of lemon juice (freshly squeezed)

- 3 cups of mint leaves (fresh, rinsed, chopped finely)

- 4 ½ cups of water

- 7 cups of sugar

Directions:

1. In a saucepan, add the water and mint leaves over medium heat. Stir well and bring the mixture to a boil.

2. Once the mixture starts boiling, take the saucepan off the heat.

3. Use a lid to cover the saucepan and allow to rest for about 10 minutes.

4. After resting, pour the mixture into a fine mesh strainer placed over a bowl.

5. Squeeze and press the leaves to get all of the liquid, then discard the leaves.

6. Prepare the jars by heating them up in the water bath canner. Heat up the water in the canner, but not to the point of boiling.

7. In a pot, add the mint liquid, pectin, and lemon juice over medium heat. Stir everything together and bring the mixture to a boil.

8. Add the sugar and whisk occasionally until the sugar dissolves. Bring the mixture to a rolling boil.

9. Allow to boil for about 1 to 2 minutes, then take the pot off the heat.

10. Take the pot off the heat and use a spoon to remove any foam on the top.

11. Use a ladle and a funnel to spoon the jelly into the jars making sure that there is ¼-inch of headspace.

12. Remove the air bubbles and add more jelly as needed.

13. Wipe the rims of the jars clean, then place the seal and ring.

14. Add the jars to the water bath canner, then bring the canner to a boil.

15. Once the water is boiling, cover the water bath canner and process based on your altitude:

    a) 5 minutes for altitudes between 0 and 1,000 feet

    b) 10 minutes for altitudes between 1,001 and 6,000 feet

    c) 15 minutes for altitudes above 6,001 feet

16. After processing, turn off the heat and take the lid off the canner.

17. Allow to rest for about 5 minutes before taking the jars out of the hot water.

18. Place the jars on a thick kitchen towel and allow them to cool down for up to 24 hours.

19. Remove the jars, check the seals, label, and store.

SPICY PEPPER JELLY

This jelly has just the right kick to it as it combines sweet and spicy peppers. Layer it over cheese for a perfect pairing!

Time: 40 minutes

Serving Size: 3-pint jars

Prep Time: 30 minutes

Processing Time: 10 minutes

Ingredients:

- ½ tsp fine sea salt

- 3 tbsp fruit pectin

- 1 cup of honey

- 1 cup of jalapeño pepper (finely chopped)

- 1 ¼ cups of apple cider vinegar

- 2 cups of sugar (preferably organic)

- 4 cups of red, yellow, and green bell peppers (finely chopped)

Directions:

1. Prepare the jars by heating them up in the water bath canner. Heat up the water in the canner, but not to the point of boiling.

2. In a pot, add the apple cider vinegar, bell peppers, and jalapeño pepper over high heat.

3. Gradually add the pectin while stirring gently, then bring the mixture to a boil. Allow to boil for about 1 to 2 minutes.

4. Add the honey and sugar. Stir well until the sugar dissolves, then return the mixture to a rolling boil.

5. Allow to boil for about 3 minutes while stirring constantly.

6. Take the pot off the heat. Stir the salt into the jelly, then use a spoon to remove any foam on the top.

7. Use a ladle and a funnel to spoon the jelly into the jars making sure that there is ¼-inch of headspace.

8. Remove the air bubbles and add more jelly as needed.

9. Wipe the rims of the jars clean, then place the seal and ring.

10. Add the jars to the water bath canner, then bring the canner to a boil.

11. Once the water is boiling, cover the water bath canner and process for 10 minutes.

12. After processing, turn off the heat and take the lid off the canner.

13. Allow to rest for about 5 minutes before taking the jars out of the hot water.

14. Place the jars on a thick kitchen towel and allow them to cool down for up to 24 hours.

15. Remove the jars, check the seals, label, and store.

WATERMELON JELLY

This jelly has a very vibrant color and an intense flavor. Whip it up so that you can enjoy the fresh summer flavor no matter what the season.

Time: 40 minutes

Serving Size: 3-pint jars

Prep Time: 30 minutes

Processing Time: 10 minutes

Ingredients:

- ¼ cup of lemon juice (freshly squeezed)

- ⅓ cup of white wine vinegar

- ¾ cup of fruit pectin (liquid)

- 5 cups of sugar

- 6 cups of watermelon (seeds removed, chopped)

Directions:

1. In a food processor, add the watermelon, and process into a purée.

2. Place a fine-mesh sieve on top of a bowl, then cover it with 4 sheets of cheesecloth.

3. Pour the watermelon purée into the sieve. Allow to stand for about 10 minutes or until you get about 2 cups of watermelon juice.

4. Prepare the jars by heating them up in the water bath canner. Heat up the water in the canner, but not to the point of boiling.

5. In a pot, add the watermelon juice, vinegar, sugar, and lemon juice over high heat.

6. Stir everything together and bring the mixture to a boil. Allow to boil for about 1 to 2 minutes while stirring constantly.

7. Add the pectin and continue to boil for about 1 minute while stirring constantly.

8. Take the pot off the heat and use a spoon to remove any foam on the top.

9. Use a ladle and a funnel to spoon the jelly into the jars making sure that there is ¼-inch of headspace.

10. Remove the air bubbles and add more jelly as needed.

11. Wipe the rims of the jars clean, then place the seal and ring.

12. Add the jars to the water bath canner, then bring the canner to a boil.

13. Once the water is boiling, cover the water bath canner and process for 10 minutes.

14. After processing, turn off the heat and take the lid off the canner.

15. Allow to rest for about 5 minutes before taking the jars out of the hot water.

16. Place the jars on a thick kitchen towel and allow them to cool down for up to 24 hours.

17. Remove the jars, check the seals, label, and store.

Chapter 8

RECIPES FOR CANNING SALSAS AND SAUCES

Salsas and sauces make your meals more interesting. You can pair them with different dishes, which means that having these preserves in your pantry is a must! Here are some simply yet scrumptious salsa and sauce recipes for you to start with.

APPLE AND PEACH SALSA

Combining these two fruits creates a stunning salsa that's subtly sweet and flavorful. Serve it with various dishes to add a fresh and bright sweet flavor.

Time: depends on the altitude

Serving Size: 7-pint jars

Prep Time: 30 minutes

Processing Time: depends on the altitude

Ingredients:

- 2 tsp red pepper flakes

- 1 tbsp canning salt

- 4 tbsp mixed pickling spice

- 2 cups of Granny Smith apples (chopped)

- 2 cups of green bell peppers (seeds removed, chopped)

- 2 ¼ cups cider vinegar (preferably 5%)

- 2 ½ cups of yellow onions (diced)

- 3 ¾ cups of packed light brown sugar

- 6 cups of Roma tomatoes (rinsed, peeled, chopped)

- 8 cups of ascorbic acid solution (⅔ tsp of ascorbic acid mixed with 8 cups of water)

- 10 cups of peaches (hard, unripe, chopped)

Directions:

1. In a bowl, add the apples, peaches, and ascorbic acid solution. Mix well and soak the fruits for about 10 minutes.

2. Layer 2 small sheets of cheesecloth and place the pickling spice in the middle.

3. Wrap the pickling spice by bringing the corners of the cheesecloth together, then tie them up with a piece of string. Set aside.

4. In a pot, add the tomatoes, onion, and bell peppers over medium heat.

5. After soaking, discard the liquid, and add the fruits to the pot.

6. Add the spice bag, vinegar, sugar, red pepper flakes, and salt. Stir everything together and bring the mixture to a boil.

7. Once the mixture starts boiling, turn the heat down to low. Allow to simmer for about 30 minutes while stirring occasionally.

8. Prepare the jars by heating them up in the water bath canner. Heat up the water in the canner, but not to the point of boiling.

9. After simmering, use a slotted spoon to take the spice bag out of the pot.

10. Use a ladle and a funnel to spoon the salsa into the jars making sure that there is 1 ¼-inch of headspace.

11. Remove the air bubbles and add more salsa as needed.

12. Wipe the rims of the jars clean, then place the seal and ring.

13. Add the jars to the water bath canner, then bring the canner to a boil.

14. Once the water is boiling, cover the water bath canner and process based on your altitude:

    a) 15 minutes for altitudes between 0 and 1,000 feet

    b) 20 minutes for altitudes between 1,001 and 6,000 feet

    c) 25 minutes for altitudes above 6,001 feet

15. After processing, turn off the heat and take the lid off the canner.

16. Allow to rest for about 5 minutes before taking the jars out of the hot water.

17. Place the jars on a thick kitchen towel and allow them to cool down for up to 24 hours.

18. Remove the jars, check the seals, label, and store.

CLASSIC TOMATO SALSA

When it comes to salsa, tomatoes are the most common ingredient used. Here is a simple recipe for you to make classic tomato salsa with some fresh chilies.

Time: depends on the altitude

Serving Size: 5-pint jars

Prep Time: 30 minutes

Processing Time: depends on the altitude

Ingredients:

- ½ tsp cumin (ground)

- 2 tsp oregano (dried)

- 2 tsp salt

- 2 tbsp sugar

- ½ cup cilantro (fresh, loosely packed, chopped)

- 1 cup of Anaheim green chilies (roasted, peeled, chopped)

- 1 cup of apple cider vinegar

- 1 ½ cups of onion (chopped)

- 7 cups of tomatoes (blanched, grilled, or boiled, peeled, chopped)

- 3 cloves of garlic (minced)

- 3 jalapeños (seeds and stems removed, chopped)

Directions:

1. Prepare the jars by heating them up in the water bath canner. Heat up the water in the canner, but not to the point of boiling.

2. In a pot, add all of the ingredients over medium heat. Stir everything together and bring the mixture to a boil.

3. Once the mixture starts to boil, turn the heat down to low. Allow to simmer for about 10 minutes.

4. Use a ladle and a funnel to spoon the salsa into the jars making sure that there is ½-inch of headspace.

5. Remove the air bubbles and add more salsa as needed.

6. Wipe the rims of the jars clean, then place the seal and ring.

7. Add the jars to the water bath canner, then bring the canner to a boil.

8. Once the water is boiling, cover the water bath canner and process based on your altitude:

   a) 15 minutes for altitudes between 0 and 1,000 feet

   b) 20 minutes for altitudes between 1,001 and 6,000 feet

   c) 25 minutes for altitudes above 6,001 feet

9. After processing, turn off the heat and take the lid off the canner.

10. Allow to rest for about 5 minutes before taking the jars out of the hot water.

11. Place the jars on a thick kitchen towel and allow them to cool down for up to 24 hours.

12. Remove the jars, check the seals, label, and store.

ROASTED SPICY SALSA

If you like your salsa with a little kick, then this is the perfect recipe for you. It's easy to make and it packs a lot of flavor!

Time: 50 minutes

Serving Size: 6-pint jars

Prep Time: 40 minutes

Processing Time: 10 minutes

Ingredients:

- ½ tsp black pepper (ground)

- 1 ½ tsp chili powder

- 2 tsp cumin (ground)

- 2 ½ tsp espresso powder

- 3 tsp kosher salt

- ½ cup of cilantro (fresh, chopped)

- 1 cup of apple cider vinegar

- 2 ¼ cups of white onions (diced)

- 4 ½ cups of peppers (a combination of green bell peppers, red bell peppers, and jalapeños, rinsed, dried)

- 5 ½ cups of heirloom or regular tomatoes (rinsed, dried)

- 5 ¾ cups of Roma tomatoes (rinsed, dried)

- 5 cloves of garlic

Directions:

1. Set your oven to broil.

2. In a sheet pan, add the tomatoes and peppers, then spread them out in one layer.

3. Place the sheet pan in the oven. Broil the vegetables until their skin starts to blister.

4. Turn the vegetables over and continue broiling until the skins start to blister.

5. Take the sheet pan out of the oven and allow the vegetables to cool down slightly.

6. When the peppers are cool enough to handle, chop them.

7. Prepare the jars by heating them up in the water bath canner. Heat up the water in the canner, but not to the point of boiling.

8. In a blender, add the tomatoes (along with the juices in the sheet pan), garlic, and half of the onions. Blend until you get a relatively smooth texture.

9. In a pot, add the blended vegetables along with the rest of the ingredients over medium heat. Stir everything well and bring the mixture to a boil.

10. Once the mixture starts to boil, turn the heat down to low. Allow to simmer for about 10 minutes while stirring occasionally.

11. Use a ladle and a funnel to spoon the salsa into the jars making sure that there is ½-inch of headspace.

12. Remove the air bubbles and add more salsa as needed.

13. Wipe the rims of the jars clean, then place the seal and ring.

14. Add the jars to the water bath canner, then bring the canner to a boil.

15. Once the water is boiling, cover the water bath canner and process for 15 minutes.

16. After processing, turn off the heat and take the lid off the canner.

17. Allow to rest for about 5 minutes before taking the jars out of the hot water.

18. Place the jars on a thick kitchen towel and allow them to cool down for up to 24 hours.

19. Remove the jars, check the seals, label, and store.

SALSA VERDE

Make this mouthwatering salsa using fresh tomatillos and other ingredients. This salsa goes well with various dishes making it a great addition to your prepper pantry.

Time: 50 minutes

Serving Size: 4-pint jars

Prep Time: 35 minutes

Processing Time: 15 minutes

Ingredients:

- 2 tsp smoked Spanish paprika

- 3 tsp kosher salt

- 2 tbsp cumin

- 6 tbsp lime juice (freshly squeezed)

- ⅔ cup of cilantro (fresh, minced)

- 1 cup of white vinegar

- 2 cups of onion (chopped)

- 2 cups of peppers (a combination of green bell peppers, Thai chilies, and jalapeños, chopped)

- 11 cups of tomatillos (husked, cores removed, chopped)

- 12 cloves of garlic (minced)

Directions:

1. Preheat your oven to 500 °F.

2. On a baking sheet, add ¾ of the tomatillos and arrange them in one layer.

281

3. Place the baking sheet in the oven. Roast the tomatillos for about 20 minutes until slightly charred.

4. After roasting, take the baking sheet out of the oven. Allow the tomatillos to cool down slightly.

5. Prepare the jars by heating them up in the water bath canner. Heat up the water in the canner, but not to the point of boiling.

6. In a food processor, add the peppers and onion. Pulse until roughly chopped.

7. Transfer the chopped vegetables to a pot.

8. Add the raw and roasted tomatillos to the food processor. Pulse for a few seconds until roughly chopped.

9. Add the tomatillos to the pot along with the rest of the ingredients except for the cilantro.

10. Place the pot on the stove over medium heat. Stir everything well and bring the mixture to a boil.

11. Once the mixture starts to boil, turn the heat down to low. Allow to simmer for about 11 minutes.

12. Add the cilantro, mix well, and continue simmering for about 1 minute more.

13. Use a ladle and a funnel to spoon the salsa into the jars making sure that there is ½-inch of headspace.

14. Remove the air bubbles and add more salsa as needed.

15. Wipe the rims of the jars clean, then place the seal and ring.

16. Add the jars to the water bath canner, then bring the canner to a boil.

17. Once the water is boiling, cover the water bath canner and process for 15 minutes.

18. After processing, turn off the heat and take the lid off the canner.

19. Allow to rest for about 5 minutes before taking the jars out of the hot water.

20. Place the jars on a thick kitchen towel and allow them to cool down for up to 24 hours.

21. Remove the jars, check the seals, label, and store.

SWEET STRAWBERRY SALSA

Have you ever tried sweet salsa? This salsa has a gorgeous vibrant color and the perfect combination of sweet, spicy, and fresh flavors.

Time: 50 minutes

Serving Size: 7-pint jars

Prep Time: 30 minutes

Processing Time: 20 minutes

Ingredients:

- 1 tsp sea salt

- ¼ cup of mint (fresh, finely chopped)

- ½ cup of agave sweetener

- ½ cup of cilantro (fresh, chopped)

- ½ cup of green bell pepper (stems and seeds removed, diced)

- ½ cup of lime juice (freshly squeezed)

- ¾ cup of red bell pepper (stems and seeds removed, diced)

- 1 cup of jalapeño (seeds removed, finely chopped)

- 1 cup of red onion (diced)

- 1 ¼ cups of apple cider vinegar

- 1 ¼ cups of Vidalia onions (diced)

- 5 cups of sugar (granulated)

- 12 cups of strawberries (stems removed, chopped)

Directions:

1. Prepare the jars by heating them up in the water bath canner. Heat up the water in the canner, but not to the point of boiling.

2. In a pot, add the sweetener, sugar, and vinegar over medium-high heat. Stir everything together until the sugar dissolves.

3. Add the lime juice, herbs, onions, peppers, and peppers. Stir everything together and bring the mixture to a boil.

4. Allow the mixture to boil for about 5 minutes before taking the pot off the heat.

5. Fold the strawberries into the mixture making sure to coat all of the fruit pieces completely.

6. Use a ladle and a funnel to spoon the salsa into the jars making sure that there is ½-inch of headspace.

7. Remove the air bubbles and add more salsa as needed.

8. Wipe the rims of the jars clean, then place the seal and ring.

9. Add the jars to the water bath canner, then bring the canner to a boil.

10. Once the water is boiling, cover the water bath canner and process for 20 minutes.

11. After processing, turn off the heat and take the lid off the canner.

12. Allow to rest for about 5 minutes before taking the jars out of the hot water.

13. Place the jars on a thick kitchen towel and allow them to cool down for up to 24 hours.

14. Remove the jars, check the seals, label, and store.

BARBEQUE SAUCE

Make your own barbeque sauce at home to enjoy with meat, chicken, and other grilled foods. This is another simple recipe that belongs in your stockpile.

Time: depends on the altitude

Serving Size: 4-pint jars

Prep Time: 3 hours, 15 minutes

Processing Time: depends on the altitude

Ingredients:

- 1 tsp black peppercorns

- 1 tsp hot pepper sauce

- 1 ¼ tsp cayenne pepper

- 1 tbsp canning salt

- 1 tbsp dry mustard

- 1 tbsp paprika

- 1 cup of brown sugar

- 1 ¼ cups of vinegar (preferably 5%)

- 1 ½ cups of red bell peppers (stem and seeds removed, chopped)

- 2 cups of celery (fresh, chopped)

- 2 cups of onions (chopped)

- 16 cups of tomatoes (peeled, cored, chopped)

- 2 cloves of garlic (crushed)

- 2 hot red peppers (stem and seeds removed, chopped)

Directions:

1. In a pot, add the celery, peppers, onions, and tomatoes over medium heat. Mix everything well and cook for about 30 minutes until the vegetables are soft.

2. Transfer the softened vegetables to a blender, then purée until smooth.

3. Pour the mixture back into the pot and cook for about 45 minutes until it reduces by half.

4. Layer 2 small sheets of cheesecloth and place the peppercorns in the middle.

5. Wrap the peppercorns by bringing the corners of the cheesecloth together, then tie them up with a piece of string.

6. Add the bag to the pot along with the rest of the ingredients.

7. Mix everything well and cook for about 1 ½ to 2 hours until the mixture thickens into a sauce. Stir frequently while cooking.

8. Prepare the jars by heating them up in the water bath canner. Heat up the water in the canner, but not to the point of boiling.

9. Use a slotted spoon to remove the bag of peppercorns from the pot of sauce.

10. Use a ladle and a funnel to spoon the sauce into the jars making sure that there is ½-inch of headspace.

11. Remove the air bubbles and add more sauce as needed.

12. Wipe the rims of the jars clean, then place the seal and ring.

13. Add the jars to the water bath canner, then bring the canner to a boil.

14. Once the water is boiling, cover the water bath canner and process based on your altitude:

    a) 20 minutes for altitudes between 0 and 1,000 feet

    b) 25 minutes for altitudes between 1,001 and 3,000 feet

    c) 30 minutes for altitudes between 3,001 and 6,000 feet

    d) 35 minutes for altitudes above 6,001 feet

15. After processing, turn off the heat and take the lid off the canner.

16. Allow to rest for about 5 minutes before taking the jars out of the hot water.

17. Place the jars on a thick kitchen towel and allow them to cool down for up to 24 hours.

18. Remove the jars, check the seals, label, and store.

CHOCOLATE AND RASPBERRY SAUCE

Chocolate and raspberries go so well together. In this recipe, you will make a delicious sauce that pairs perfectly with cake, ice cream, and other sweet treats.

Time: 25 minutes

Serving Size: 3-pint jars

Prep Time: 15 minutes

Processing Time: 10 minutes

Ingredients:

- 3 ½ tbsp pectin (powdered)

- 4 tbsp lemon juice (freshly squeezed)

- ½ cup of cocoa powder (unsweetened)

- 4 ½ cups red raspberries (fresh, crushed)

- 6 ¾ cups of sugar (granulated)

Directions:

1. Prepare the jars by heating them up in the water bath canner. Heat up the water in the canner, but not to the point of boiling.

2. In a bowl, add the pectin powder and cocoa. Mix well and set aside.

3. In a saucepan, add the lemon juice and raspberries over medium heat. Mix until well combined.

4. Whisk the cocoa mixture into the raspberry mixture.

5. Turn the heat up to high, then bring the mixture to a rolling boil while stirring frequently.

6. Once the mixture starts boiling, add the sugar.

7. Mix everything together until the sugar dissolves completely, then bring to a rolling boil while stirring frequently.

8. Continue boiling for about 1 minute before removing the saucepan from the heat.

9. Use a spoon to remove any foam on the top.

10. Use a ladle and a funnel to spoon the sauce into the jars making sure that there is ¼-inch of headspace.

11. Remove the air bubbles and add more sauce as needed.

12. Wipe the rims of the jars clean, then place the seal and ring.

13. Add the jars to the water bath canner, then bring the canner to a boil.

14. Once the water is boiling, cover the water bath canner and process for 10 minutes.

15. After processing, turn off the heat and take the lid off the canner.

16. Allow to rest for about 5 minutes before taking the jars out of the hot water.

17. Place the jars on a thick kitchen towel and allow them to cool down for up to 24 hours.

18. Remove the jars, check the seals, label, and store.

PEAR SAUCE WITH VANILLA AND CARAMEL

Here is another sweet sauce for you to try. Combining pears with caramel and vanilla results in a smooth and tasty outcome.

Time: 25 minutes

Serving Size: 4-pint jars

Prep Time: 15 minutes

Processing Time: 10 minutes

Ingredients:

- 2 tsp sea salt

- 4 tsp vanilla bean paste

- 3 cups of water

- 6 cups of sugar (granulated)

- 9 cups of pears (cored, chopped)

Directions:

1. Prepare the jars by heating them up in the water bath canner. Heat up the water in the canner, but not to the point of boiling.

2. In a blender, add the pears, salt, vanilla bean paste, and ¼ cup of water. Blend until you get a smooth purée.

3. In a saucepan, add the sugar and 1 ½ cups of water over high heat. Stir well and bring the mixture to a boil.

4. Once the mixture starts to boil, turn the heat down to medium-high. Allow to simmer for about 15 to 20 minutes.

5. After simmering, take the pan off the heat. Add the pear purée and mix well.

6. Place the pot back on the heat until you get the desired consistency.

7. Use a ladle and a funnel to spoon the sauce into the jars making sure that there is ¼-inch of headspace.

8. Remove the air bubbles and add more sauce as needed.

9. Wipe the rims of the jars clean, then place the seal and ring.

10. Add the jars to the water bath canner, then bring the canner to a boil.

11. Once the water is boiling, cover the water bath canner and process for 10 minutes.

12. After processing, turn off the heat and take the lid off the canner.

13. Allow to rest for about 5 minutes before taking the jars out of the hot water.

14. Place the jars on a thick kitchen towel and allow them to cool down for up to 24 hours.

15. Remove the jars, check the seals, label, and store.

PIZZA SAUCE

Nothing beats homemade pizza. Learn how to make this tasty sauce to slather onto your crust before adding all of your favorite toppings.

Time: 2 hours, 25 minutes

Serving Size: 7-pint jars

Prep Time: 2 hours

Processing Time: 25 minutes

Ingredients:

- 2 tsp peppercorns (cracked)
- 2 tsp rosemary (fresh, chopped)
- 2 tsp sea salt
- 2 tbsp basil (fresh, chopped)
- 2 tbsp oregano
- 2 tbsp sugar
- 4 tbsp parsley (fresh, chopped)
- 6 tbsp olive oil
- 7 tbsp lemon juice (freshly squeezed)
- 3 cups of onions (minced)
- 28 ¾ cups of Roma tomatoes (peeled)
- 4 cloves of garlic (minced)

Directions:

1. In a blender, add the tomatoes and purée until smooth.

2. In a stock pot, add the olive oil, onions, and garlic over medium heat. Sauté for about 4 to 5 minutes until tender and translucent.

3. Add the tomato purée and mix well.

4. Add the rest of the ingredients except for the lemon juice. Stir everything together and bring the mixture to a boil.

5. Once the mixture starts to boil, turn the heat down to medium-low. Allow to simmer for about 2 hours while stirring occasionally.

6. Prepare the jars by heating them up in the water bath canner. Heat up the water in the canner, but not to the point of boiling.

7. When the pizza sauce has reached your desired consistency, add 1 tablespoon of lemon juice to each of the jars.

8. Use a ladle and a funnel to spoon the sauce into the jars making sure that there is ½-inch of headspace.

9. Remove the air bubbles and add more sauce as needed.

10. Wipe the rims of the jars clean, then place the seal and ring.

11. Add the jars to the water bath canner, then bring the canner to a boil.

12. Once the water is boiling, cover the water bath canner and process for 25 minutes.

13. After processing, turn off the heat and take the lid off the canner.

14. Allow to rest for about 5 minutes before taking the jars out of the hot water.

15. Place the jars on a thick kitchen towel and allow them to cool down for up to 24 hours.

16. Remove the jars, check the seals, label, and store.

SPICY PEPPER SAUCE

Use this spicy sauce in tacos, pasta, soup, sandwiches, and anything else you want to add a kick to! It's very tasty and easy to make.

Time: depends on the altitude

Serving Size: 4-pint jars

Prep Time: 50 minutes

Processing Time: depends on the altitude

Ingredients:

- ½ tsp allspice (ground)

- ½ tsp cloves (ground)

- 1 tsp cumin (ground)

- 1 tsp garlic powder

- 1 tsp mustard (ground)

- 1 tsp sea salt

- 1 tsp turmeric (ground)

- 4 tsp sugar

- 1 cup of apple cider vinegar

- 1 cup of onion (chopped)

- 1 cup of white vinegar

- 2 ¼ cups of peppers (a mixture of hot and sweet peppers, sliced)

Directions:

1. In a stockpot, add the white vinegar, apple cider vinegar, cumin, turmeric, allspice, sugar, mustard, clove, salt, sugar, garlic powder, onion, and peppers over medium heat. Stir everything together and bring the mixture to a simmer.

2. Once the mixture starts to simmer, use a lid to cover the stockpot. Allow to simmer for about 20 minutes.

3. Prepare the jars by heating them up in the water bath canner. Heat up the water in the canner, but not to the point of boiling.

4. After simmering, transfer the mixture to a blender. Purée until you get a smooth and thick consistency.

5. Use a ladle and a funnel to spoon the sauce into the jars making sure that there is ¼-inch of headspace.

6. Remove the air bubbles and add more sauce as needed.

7. Wipe the rims of the jars clean, then place the seal and ring.

8. Add the jars to the water bath canner, then bring the canner to a boil.

9. Once the water is boiling, cover the water bath canner and process based on your altitude:

    a) 10 minutes for altitudes between 0 and 1,000 feet

    b) 15 minutes for altitudes between 1,001 and 3,000 feet

    c) 20 minutes for altitudes between 3,001 and 6,000 feet

    d) 25 minutes for altitudes above 6,001 feet

10. After processing, turn off the heat and take the lid off the canner.

11. Allow to rest for about 5 minutes before taking the jars out of the hot water.

12. Place the jars on a thick kitchen towel and allow them to cool down for up to 24 hours.

13. Remove the jars, check the seals, label, and store.

Chapter 9

OTHER CANNING RECIPES TO TRY

As a beginner in water bath canning, you can experiment with different recipes that have varying levels of complexities. Doing this will make you feel more confident in your canning abilities. In this chapter, you will learn how to make condiments, pie fillings, and more!

KETCHUP

Ketchup is a very common condiment that you can use with different dishes. Make your own ketchup at home and add it to your stockpile.

Time: 45 minutes

Serving Size: 3-pint jars

Prep Time: 30 minutes

Processing Time: 15 minutes

Ingredients:

- 1 tsp allspice (ground)

- 1 tsp black pepper (finely ground)

- 1 tsp celery seed

- 1 tsp cinnamon (ground)

- 1 tsp cloves (ground)

- 1 tsp garlic powder

- 2 tsp ginger (fresh, minced)

- 3 tbsp sea salt

- ½ cup of cane sugar (unrefined, you can also use palm sugar)

- 1 ½ cups of apple cider vinegar

- 2 cups of yellow onion (diced)

- 23 cups of plum tomatoes (chopped)

Directions:

1. In a stockpot, add the onions and tomatoes over medium-high heat. Stir the vegetables together and bring the mixture to a boil.

2. Continue boiling while stirring frequently until the juices are reduced by half.

3. Pour the cooked vegetables into a fine mesh sieve placed over a bowl.

4. Use a spoon to mash the vegetables to separate the liquids from the seeds and skins.

5. Prepare the jars by heating them up in the water bath canner. Heat up the water in the canner, but not to the point of boiling.

6. Pour the vegetable liquid back into the stockpot.

7. Add the sugar, vinegar, sea salt, and all of the spices. Stir everything together and bring the mixture to a gentle boil.

8. Continue boiling until you get the desired ketchup consistency.

9. Use a ladle and a funnel to spoon the ketchup into the jars making sure that there is ½-inch of headspace.

10. Remove the air bubbles and add more ketchup as needed.

11. Wipe the rims of the jars clean, then place the seal and ring.

12. Add the jars to the water bath canner, then bring the canner to a boil.

13. Once the water is boiling, cover the water bath canner and process for 15 minutes.

14. After processing, turn off the heat and take the lid off the canner.

15. Allow to rest for about 5 minutes before taking the jars out of the hot water.

16. Place the jars on a thick kitchen towel and allow them to cool down for up to 24 hours.

17. Remove the jars, check the seals, label, and store.

WHOLEGRAIN MUSTARD

While jams and jellies are easy to prepare and you can consume them immediately. But for mustard, you need to wait for at least one month for the flavors to mellow out.

Time: 30 minutes (soaking time not included)

Serving Size: 3-pint jars

Prep Time: 20 minutes

Processing Time: 10 minutes

Ingredients:

- 2 tsp salt

- ½ cup of brown mustard seeds

- ½ cup of yellow mustard seeds

- ⅔ cup of water

- 1 ½ cups of apple cider vinegar

Directions:

1. In a jar with a lid, add all of the ingredients.

2. Mix well and allow to sit overnight for the mustard seeds to rehydrate.

3. The next day, prepare the jars by heating them up in the water bath canner. Heat up the water in the canner, but not to the point of boiling.

4. Pour the contents of the jar into a blender. Blend until you get the desired mustard consistency.

5. Pour the mustard into a saucepan over medium heat to warm it up.

6. Use a ladle and a funnel to spoon the mustard into the jars making sure that there is ½-inch of headspace.

7. Remove the air bubbles and add more mustard as needed.

8. Wipe the rims of the jars clean, then place the seal and ring.

9. Add the jars to the water bath canner, then bring the canner to a boil.

10. Once the water is boiling, cover the water bath canner and process for 10 minutes.

11. After processing, turn off the heat and take the lid off the canner.

12. Allow to rest for about 5 minutes before taking the jars out of the hot water.

13. Place the jars on a thick kitchen towel and allow them to cool down for up to 24 hours.

14. Remove the jars, check the seals, label, and store.

PICKLE RELISH

Relish is a wonderful condiment as you can use it in salads and other dishes. This recipe gives you a sweet type of relish to add to your prepper pantry.

Time: 35 minutes (soaking time not included)

Serving Size: 6-pint jars

Prep Time: 25 minutes

Processing Time: 10 minutes

Ingredients:

- 1 tbsp celery seed
- 1 tbsp mustard seed
- ¼ cup of salt
- 1 cup of green bell pepper (chopped)
- 1 cup of red bell pepper (chopped)
- 2 cups of apple cider vinegar
- 2 cups of onions (chopped)
- 3 ½ cups of sugar
- 4 cups of cucumbers (chopped)
- Water (for soaking the vegetables)

Directions:

1. In a bowl, add the bell peppers, onions, and cucumbers.
2. Add the salt and enough cold water to submerge the vegetables completely.

3. Soak the vegetables for about 2 hours.

4. After soaking, drain and discard the liquid.

5. Rinse the vegetables and drain well.

6. Prepare the jars by heating them up in the water bath canner. Heat up the water in the canner, but not to the point of boiling.

7. In a saucepan, add the vinegar, sugar, and spices over medium heat. Stir everything together and bring the mixture to a boil.

8. Once the mixture starts to boil, add the vegetables. Mix well and allow to simmer for about 10 minutes.

9. Use a ladle and a funnel to spoon the relish into the jars making sure that there is ¼-inch of headspace.

10. Remove the air bubbles and add more relish as needed.

11. Wipe the rims of the jars clean, then place the seal and ring.

12. Add the jars to the water bath canner, then bring the canner to a boil.

13. Once the water is boiling, cover the water bath canner and process for 10 minutes.

14. After processing, turn off the heat and take the lid off the canner.

15. Allow to rest for about 5 minutes before taking the jars out of the hot water.

16. Place the jars on a thick kitchen towel and allow them to cool down for up to 24 hours.

17. Remove the jars, check the seals, label, and store.

SWEET CORN RELISH

This recipe for homemade sweet corn relish will surely tantalize your taste buds. Prepare this unique and interesting relish, then add it to your stockpile.

Time: 45 minutes

Serving Size: 6-pint jars

Prep Time: 30 minutes

Processing Time: 15 minutes

Ingredients:

- 1 tbsp celery seed

- 1 tbsp mustard seed

- 1 tbsp turmeric

- 2 tbsp flour

- 2 tbsp mustard powder

- 2 tbsp salt

- 4 tbsp water

- 1 cup of onion (finely chopped)

- 1 ¼ cups of white sugar

- 1 ¾ cups of celery (finely chopped)

- 4 cups of bell pepper (finely chopped)

- 4 cups of white vinegar (preferably 5%)

- 8 cups of corn kernels

- 1 clove of garlic (minced)

Directions:

1. Prepare the jars by heating them up in the water bath canner. Heat up the water in the canner, but not to the point of boiling.

2. In a pot, add all of the ingredients except for the flour and water over medium heat.

3. Stir everything well and bring the mixture to a boil.

4. Once the mixture starts to boil, turn the heat down to low. Allow to simmer for about 10 minutes while stirring occasionally.

5. In a bowl, add the flour and water. Mix well.

6. Add 2 to 3 tablespoons of the hot mixture into the bowl and stir well.

7. Pour the mixture into the pot and stir well.

8. Allow to simmer for about 5 minutes while stirring frequently.

9. Use a ladle and a funnel to spoon the relish into the jars making sure that there is ½-inch of headspace.

10. Remove the air bubbles and add more relish as needed.

11. Wipe the rims of the jars clean, then place the seal and ring.

12. Add the jars to the water bath canner, then bring the canner to a boil.

13. Once the water is boiling, cover the water bath canner and process for 15 minutes.

14. After processing, turn off the heat and take the lid off the canner.

15. Allow to rest for about 5 minutes before taking the jars out of the hot water.

16. Place the jars on a thick kitchen towel and allow them to cool down for up to 24 hours.

17. Remove the jars, check the seals, label, and store.

APPLE PIE FILLING

Homemade apple pie is the ultimate comfort food. If you love making apple pie, it's a good idea to stock up on apple pie filling so you always have it ready when needed.

Time: 55 minutes

Serving Size: 7-pint jars

Prep Time: 30 minutes

Processing Time: 25 minutes

Ingredients:

- ½ tsp nutmeg (ground)

- 1 ½ tsp cinnamon (ground)

- ½ cup of lemon juice (freshly squeezed)

- ¾ cup of Clear Jel

- 1 ¼ cups of water

- 2 ½ cups of apple juice

- 2 ¾ cups of sugar

- 4 cups of water

- 12 cups of apples (peeled, cored, sliced, splashed with fresh lemon juice)

Directions:

1. In a pot, add the water over medium heat and bring to a boil.

2. In batches, blanch the sliced apples in the boiling water for about 1 minute.

3. Transfer the blanched apples to a bowl, then cover the bowl to keep the blanched apples warm.

4. Prepare the jars by heating them up in the water bath canner. Heat up the water in the canner, but not to the point of boiling.

5. In a saucepan, add the rest of the ingredients except for the lemon juice. Stir everything together and bring the mixture to a boil.

6. Once the mixture starts to boil, add the lemon juice. Stir well and return the mixture to a boil. Continue boiling for about 1 minute.

7. Add the sliced apples and mix well.

8. Use a ladle and a funnel to spoon the pie filling into the jars making sure that there is 1-inch of headspace.

9. Remove the air bubbles and add more pie filling as needed.

10. Wipe the rims of the jars clean, then place the seal and ring.

11. Add the jars to the water bath canner, then bring the canner to a boil.

12. Once the water is boiling, cover the water bath canner and process for 25 minutes.

13. After processing, turn off the heat and take the lid off the canner.

14. Allow to rest for about 5 minutes before taking the jars out of the hot water.

15. Place the jars on a thick kitchen towel and allow them to cool down for up to 24 hours.

16. Remove the jars, check the seals, label, and store.

SWEET PECAN PIE FILLING

Are you a fan of pecan pie? If you are, then this is the perfect recipe for you. It's wonderfully sweet with a lovely crunch from the pecans.

Time: 40 minutes

Serving Size: 4-pint jars

Prep Time: 20 minutes

Processing Time: 20 minutes

Ingredients:

- ½ tsp cinnamon (ground)

- ½ tsp ginger (ground)

- ½ tsp vanilla extract

- ¼ cup of lemon juice (bottled)

- ½ cup of Clear Jel

- 1 cup of light brown sugar

- 2 cups of sugar

- 3 ½ cups of pecan halves

- 4 cups of apple juice (unsweetened)

Directions:

1. Prepare the jars by heating them up in the water bath canner. Heat up the water in the canner, but not to the point of boiling.

2. In a saucepan, add the sugars, apple juice, Clear Jel, vanilla extract, ginger, and cinnamon over medium-high heat.

3. Stir everything together and cook until the mixture starts to bubble and become thicker. Keep whisking until it boils to ensure a smooth consistency.

4. Once the mixture starts to boil, add the lemon juice. Continue boiling for about 1 minute while stirring constantly.

5. Take the saucepan off the heat and fold the pecans into the filling.

6. Use a ladle and a funnel to spoon the pie filling into the jars making sure that there is 1-inch of headspace.

7. Remove the air bubbles and add more pie filling as needed.

8. Wipe the rims of the jars clean, then place the seal and ring.

9. Add the jars to the water bath canner, then bring the canner to a boil.

10. Once the water is boiling, cover the water bath canner and process for 20 minutes.

11. After processing, turn off the heat and take the lid off the canner.

12. Allow to rest for about 5 minutes before taking the jars out of the hot water.

13. Place the jars on a thick kitchen towel and allow them to cool down for up to 24 hours.

14. Remove the jars, check the seals, label, and store.

DATE AND BANANA CHUTNEY

Chutney is a very popular spread in India. There are many ways to make chutney and this is one of the best. It's incredibly tasty and robust!

Time: 2 hours, 10 minutes

Serving Size: 3-pint jars

Prep Time: 2 hours

Processing Time: 10 minutes

Ingredients:

- ½ tsp salt
- 1 tsp curry paste
- ½ cup of raisins (seeded)
- ½ cup of water
- 2 cups of dates (pitted, chopped)
- 2 cups of sugar
- 3 cups of apples (peeled, cored, chopped)
- 3 cups of banana (peeled, thinly sliced)
- 3 cups of cider vinegar (preferably 5%)
- 1 large lemon (zest and juice)
- 1 large orange (zest and juice)

Directions:

1. Prepare the jars by heating them up in the water bath canner. Heat up the water in the canner, but not to the point of boiling.

2. In a pot, add the zest and juice of the orange and lemon over medium heat.

3. Add the water, apples, cider vinegar, curry paste, and water. Stir everything together and bring the mixture to a boil.

4. Once the mixture starts to boil, turn the heat down to low. Allow to simmer for about 5 minutes.

5. Add the sugar, raisins, dates, and bananas. Continue simmering for about 1 hour to 1 ½ hours while stirring every 10 minutes or so until you get the thick consistency of chutney.

6. Use a ladle and a funnel to spoon the chutney into the jars making sure that there is ¼-inch of headspace.

7. Remove the air bubbles and add more chutney as needed.

8. Wipe the rims of the jars clean, then place the seal and ring.

9. Add the jars to the water bath canner, then bring the canner to a boil.

10. Once the water is boiling, cover the water bath canner and process for 10 minutes.

11. After processing, turn off the heat and take the lid off the canner.

12. Allow to rest for about 5 minutes before taking the jars out of the hot water.

13. Place the jars on a thick kitchen towel and allow them to cool down for up to 24 hours.

14. Remove the jars, check the seals, label, and store.

GREEN TOMATO CHUTNEY

Here's another easy chutney recipe for you. It's easy to make this chutney as you don't even have to peel the tomatoes as part of the prep work.

Time: depends on the altitude

Serving Size: 3-pint jars

Prep Time: 50 minutes

Processing Time: depends on the altitude

Ingredients:

- ⅛ tsp cloves (ground)

- ½ tsp allspice (ground)

- 1 tsp fennel seeds

- 1 tsp red pepper flakes

- 1 tsp salt

- 1 tbsp mustard seeds

- 2 tbsp ginger (candied, chopped)

- 1 cup of apple cider vinegar

- 1 cup of golden raisins

- 1 cup of red onion (chopped)

- 1 ¼ cups of brown sugar (packed)

- 7 cups of green tomatoes (cored, chopped)

- A pinch of nutmeg (ground)

- 1 cinnamon stick

Directions:

1. Prepare the jars by heating them up in the water bath canner. Heat up the water in the canner, but not to the point of boiling.

2. In a pot, add all of the ingredients over medium heat. Stir everything together and bring the mixture to a boil.

3. Once the mixture starts to boil, turn the heat down. Cover the pot with a lid and allow to simmer for about 45 minutes.

4. Use a ladle and a funnel to spoon the chutney into the jars making sure that there is ¼-inch of headspace.

5. Remove the air bubbles and add more chutney as needed.

6. Wipe the rims of the jars clean, then place the seal and ring.

7. Add the jars to the water bath canner, then bring the canner to a boil.

8. Once the water is boiling, cover the water bath canner and process for 15 minutes for altitudes below 1,000 feet or 20 minutes for altitudes between 1,001 and 6,000 feet.

9. After processing, turn off the heat and take the lid off the canner.

10. Allow to rest for about 5 minutes before taking the jars out of the hot water.

11. Place the jars on a thick kitchen towel and allow them to cool down for up to 24 hours.

12. Remove the jars, check the seals, label, and store.

VEGETABLE JUICE

This vegetable juice blend is tasty, refreshing, and healthy. Add this juice to your pantry so that you can have a nutrient-dense drink to boost your energy.

Time: 1 hour, 40 minutes

Serving Size: 7-liter jars

Prep Time: 1 hour

Processing Time: 40 minutes

Ingredients:

- 3 cups of mixed vegetables (a combination of peppers, onions, celery, and carrots, washed, peeled, seeded, finely chopped)

- 22 lbs tomatoes (washed, stems and cores removed)

- Lemon juice (bottled, as needed)

- Salt (as needed)

Directions:

1. Prepare the jars by heating them up in the water bath canner. Heat up the water in the canner, but not to the point of boiling.

2. Roughly chop 5 tomatoes and add them to a large pot over high heat.

3. Mash the tomatoes in the pot to release the juices, then bring the mixture to a boil.

4. Once the mixture starts to boil, chop 5 more tomatoes. Add them to the pot and start mashing.

5. Continue chopping, adding, and mashing tomatoes while making sure that the mixture keeps boiling.

6. After adding all of the tomatoes, allow to simmer for about 5 minutes.

7. Add the rest of the vegetables, mix well, and bring back to a simmer.

8. Allow to simmer for about 20 minutes to soften the vegetables.

9. Pour the mixture into a strainer placed over a bowl to remove any seeds and skins.

10. Pour the juice back into the pot, then season with salt.

11. Use a ladle and a funnel to spoon the juice into the jars making sure that there is ½-inch of headspace.

12. Add 2 tablespoons of lemon juice to each of the jars.

13. Remove the air bubbles and add more juice as needed.

14. Wipe the rims of the jars clean, then place the seal and ring.

15. Add the jars to the water bath canner, then bring the canner to a boil.

16. Once the water is boiling, cover the water bath canner and process for 40 minutes.

17. After processing, turn off the heat and take the lid off the canner.

18. Allow to rest for about 5 minutes before taking the jars out of the hot water.

19. Place the jars on a thick kitchen towel and allow them to cool down for up to 24 hours.

20. Remove the jars, check the seals, label, and store.

SAUERKRAUT

If you enjoy sauerkraut, why don't you make some at home? Here is a simple recipe for you to make a big batch of this healthy fermented dish.

Time: 40 minutes (fermenting time not included)

Serving Size: 18-pint jars

Prep Time: 20 minutes

Processing Time: 20 minutes

Ingredients:

- 1 ⅛ cups of canning salt

- 25 lbs cabbage

Directions:

1. Remove all of the outer leaves of each head of cabbage.

2. Wash the cabbages thoroughly, cut them into quarters, and remove the cores.

3. Use a knife or a shredder to shred the cabbages thinly.

4. In a bowl, add 5 pounds of shredded cabbage along with 3 tablespoons of canning salt.

5. Toss well and leave for about 10 minutes to let the leaves wilt slightly.

6. Firmly pack the cabbage into a clean pickling container. Use a wooden spoon to press down on the cabbage firmly until the juices come out.

7. Repeat the pickling steps for the rest of the cabbage.

8. Use a cheesecloth to cover the cabbage in the pickling jars. Tuck the edges into the insides of the jars to submerge the cabbage in the juices.

9. Each day, use a spoon to discard any scum that forms on the surface. Ferment the cabbage for about 3 to 6 weeks.

10. When ready to can, prepare the jars by heating them up in the water bath canner. Heat up the water in the canner, but not to the point of boiling.

11. In a pot, add the sauerkraut over medium heat, then bring to a simmer.

12. Use a ladle and a funnel to spoon the sauerkraut into the jars making sure that there is ½-inch of headspace.

13. Remove the air bubbles and add more sauerkraut as needed.

14. Wipe the rims of the jars clean, then place the seal and ring.

15. Add the jars to the water bath canner, then bring the canner to a boil.

16. Once the water is boiling, cover the water bath canner and process for 20 minutes.

17. After processing, turn off the heat and take the lid off the canner.

18. Allow to rest for about 5 minutes before taking the jars out of the hot water.

19. Place the jars on a thick kitchen towel and allow them to cool down for up to 24 hours.

20. Remove the jars, check the seals, label, and store.

Chapter 10

FOCUSING ON SAFETY

Becoming a canning pro isn't that difficult. The key is to know what you are doing so that you can get the best outcomes. As you learn how to process different types of food using water bath canning, one of the most important things you need to focus on is safety.

Your main purpose for canning is to have nutritious foods stocked in your pantry. But if you discovered that the canned foods you have stored have gone bad upon opening them, you would end up feeling disappointed. And if such a thing happened during an emergency, you might compromise your family's health and safety. Fortunately, you can easily avoid this by learning all about canning safety.

COMMON WATER BATH CANNING MISTAKES TO AVOID

As a beginner, you have a lot to learn about water bath canning. The more you practice, the more familiar you will be with the process. Simple as this process is, there are some common mistakes a lot of beginners make. Making these mistakes could potentially turn you off from the whole experience. Being aware of them can help you be more careful so that your learning journey can go smoothly.

Not Starting With High-Quality Ingredients

The great thing about water bath canning is that you can use it to preserve a wide range of foods to keep in your stockpile. But if you don't start with fresh, high-quality ingredients, you can't expect to get the best results. Before preparing or cooking your ingredients, inspect each of them first. Make sure to remove any ingredients that have signs of bruising, holes, and other imperfections. That way, you will only be filling your jars with the best ingredients.

Using a Water Bath Canner for Foods That Need to Be Pressure Canned

You already know why certain foods cannot be processed in a water bath canner. There is a risk of botulism and other bacteria growing inside the jars, which would then make the contents unsafe to eat. Make sure that the recipe you will follow includes ingredients that can be safely preserved in a water bath canner. If you're looking for recipes online after trying the recipes in this book, you can confirm the processing method either at the beginning of the recipe or near the end. Check first before you start.

Using the Wrong Size of Canning Jars

Water bath canning recipes should include the jar sizes too. Make sure to follow the correct jar sizes based on the recipe. If you don't have the right jar size, you may have to tweak the recipe a bit. Be as precise as possible when doing this. Consider investing in jars of different sizes so that you can preserve different kinds of preserved food to add to your stockpile.

Using Damaged Canning Jars

While it's okay to reuse canning jars, you need to check them first to see if they are still in pristine condition. Never use jars that have any kind of damage as they might break while you process them in the water bath. Even if they don't break during processing, you can't be sure that they will stay sealed when you store them in your pantry. So if you see any nicks or cracks on your jars, don't use them anymore.

Removing Air Bubbles With a Metal Spoon

Removing the air bubbles from your jars is a simple process. However, you shouldn't use a metal spoon to do this. Remember that the jars you fill are heated and in most cases, the contents are hot too. Using a metal spoon might cause the jars to crack, which would render them unsafe. Use the right tool for this purpose and try to do this step gently so you don't crush or mash the contents. It's also important not to skip this step as any bubbles that are trapped inside the jars will add to the headspace, which would then mess up the preservation process.

Not Adding Enough Water to the Pot

In order for the water bath canning process to work correctly, there needs to be enough water in the pot. The jars should be completely submerged in water. The water should be boiling underneath the jars and above them. Make sure that you have enough water in your pot throughout the process. If the processing time is a bit longer, it's a good idea to keep a kettle of boiling water next to your water bath canner so that you can keep adding more as needed.

Not Considering Your Altitude

The altitude might not seem like a big deal when you're cooking, but it does matter when you're preserving food through water bath canning. The reason for the varying processing times is that water boils at different temperatures depending on the altitude. So the higher your altitude is, the longer the processing time should be. If you don't know your altitude, you can find out using an online search. Then you can adjust your processing times accordingly.

Taking the Jars Out of the Canner Right After Processing

As you may notice in all of the recipes in this book, you should wait for five minutes after processing before taking the jars out of the canner. After processing, take the lid off the pot, then allow the jars to cool down for a bit. This helps ensure that the seals stay in place and the contents won't seep out of the jars.

Storing the Jars Without Removing the Rings

It's important to remove the rings from the lids to make sure that your jars have sealed properly. If you don't do this, it might look like your jars are sealed well but when they cool down, the seals will break. After removing the lids and allowing the jars to completely cool down, try to lift the lid to check if it will stay in place.

Not Labeling Your Jars

Labeling your jars is extremely important, especially if you will store them in your prepper pantry. You know the importance of rotating your stocks and being aware of the expiration dates. Writing down the processing dates of your stocks will make it easier to keep track of everything in your pantry. Keep doing this each time you process a new batch of preserves.

As you can see, these mistakes are very easy to rectify. Although many beginners commit these mistakes, you don't have to since you are already aware of them. Now you can focus on learning how to properly use your water bath canner to process different types of food at home.

ESSENTIAL SAFETY TIPS TO KEEP IN MIND

When done properly, water bath canning is a safe and simple process that yields wonderful results. Now that you know the common mistakes to avoid while water bath canning, let's go through some final safety tips to complete the knowledge you need to start your learning journey:

- When purchasing tools and equipment, focus on quality. Think of these purchases as an investment for your future food security.

- Use the right tools to ensure that you process your foods safely. For instance, use a jar lifter to take the jars out of the canner after processing. If you don't have a jar lifter, you may use a pair of tongs. Use whatever you have at home, but consider purchasing any tools you are lacking, especially if you plan to keep stocking your pantry with home-canned food.

- Before you start the canning process, make sure to have all of your ingredients and tools on hand. Having to search for items in your kitchen may cause delays, which could compromise the final outcome of the process.

- Always check your jars before and after processing. Do this to make sure that they didn't incur any damage during processing.

- As time goes by, keep yourself updated in terms of water bath canning. Over time, this process may evolve, which means that there might be new guidelines you would have to learn to improve and simplify the process even more.

Finally, if you open a jar of home-canned food that has been sitting on the shelf for a number of months and you smell something off, discard the jar and its contents. By keeping all of these safety tips in mind, you can start water bath canning with confidence and enjoy the results when you're done!

Conclusion

WATER BATH CANNING LIKE A PRO

Water bath canning is a simple and easy process. As long as you focus on safety, it will be a sustainable part of your life. From the beginning of this book, you discovered all of the fundamentals of canning using a water bath.

We started by defining what water bath canning is, how it works, and how it differs from other canning methods. You also learned the many benefits of this preservation method to help you understand why it is very popular. We also discussed the possible risks of this process to give you a holistic understanding of water bath canning.

The next chapter presented you with lists of the best and worst foods to preserve through this canning method. Simply put, you can only preserve high-acid foods through water bath canning. Low-acid foods aren't suitable for this method as the process doesn't reach the right temperature to kill various bacteria that cause food spoilage.

Then we moved on to some beginner tips to help you start your canning journey. In Chapter 3, you discovered the basic equipment needed along with the steps on how to start water bath canning. Before moving on to the recipes, you were also presented with valuable information about starting your own prepper pantry and meal planning routine.

These topics will help you see the true importance of food preservation through water bath canning.

Chapters 5-9 contained various canning recipes for you to start with. Try these recipes out to learn how truly simple water bath canning is. In the last chapter, you were presented with the common canning mistakes to avoid along with some important safety tips to keep in mind.

Now that you understand how water bath canning works and how to do it, it's time to start planning. Decide which recipes to try first, then go from there. Happy canning!

References

APA Adamant, A. (2018b, July 7). *How to can mango*. Practical Self Reliance. https://practicalselfreliance.com/canning-mango/

Adamant, A. (2018e, December 16). *Canning blackberries*. Practical Self Reliance. https://practicalselfreliance.com/canning-blackberries/

Adamant, A. (2019b, May 28). *Canning asparagus*. Practical Self Reliance. https://practicalselfreliance.com/canning-asparagus/

Adamant, A. (2020a, May 21). *Dandelion jelly*. Practical Self Reliance. https://practicalselfreliance.com/dandelion-jelly/

Adamant, A. (2020c, September 1). *Canning grapes*. Practical Self Reliance. https://practicalselfreliance.com/canning-grapes/

Adamant, A. (2020d, November 5). *12 Common beginner canning mistakes (And how to fix them)*. Practical Self Reliance. https://practicalselfreliance.com/beginner-canning-mistakes/

Adamant, A. (2020e, November 23). *Beginners guide to water bath canning*. Practical Self Reliance. https://practicalselfreliance.com/water-bath-canning-beginners/

Adamant, A. (2020g, December 9). *Canning whole cranberries*. Practical Self Reliance. https://practicalselfreliance.com/canning-cranberries/

Adamant, A. (2022b, June 10). *Corn cob jelly*. Creative Canning. https://creativecanning.com/corn-cob-jelly/

Adina. (2020, June 29). *How to preserve raspberries (Canning raspberries)*. Where Is My Spoon. https://whereismyspoon.co/how-to-preserve-raspberries-canning-raspberries/

allinajar2012. (2013, April 12). *How does water bath canning work*. All in a Jar. https://allinajar.com/2013/04/12/how-does-water-bath-canning-work/

Almanac. (n.d.-a). *Recipe for pickled green beans*. https://www.almanac.com/recipe/pickled-green-beans

Almanac. (n.d.-b). *Recipe for zucchini marmalade.* https://www.almanac.com/recipe/zucchini-marmalade

Amanda. (2011, September 10). *Canning salsa verde, made with tomatillos.* Heartbeet Kitchen. https://heartbeetkitchen.com/tomatillosalsaverde/

Amanda. (2013, September 12). *Fiery roasted salsa: A canning recipe!* Heartbeet Kitchen. https://heartbeetkitchen.com/fiery-roasted-salsa/

Ames, M. (2019, March 13). *Rules for safe water bath canning.* Countryside. https://www.iamcountryside.com/canning-kitchen/rules-for-safe-water-bath-canning/

Ann. (2022, May 31). *Sweet pickle relish canning recipe.* Premeditated Leftovers. https://premeditatedleftovers.com/recipes-cooking-tips/sweet-pickle-relish-canning-recipe/

Ball Mason Jars. (n.d.). *How to can: A beginner's guide.* https://www.ballmasonjars.com/canning-and-preserving-101.html

Bauer, E. (2022a, June 14). *Salsa recipe for canning {how to can salsa!}.* Simply Recipes. https://www.simplyrecipes.com/recipes/canned_tomato_salsa/

Belk, M. (2013, May 9). *Canning kiwifruit.* Thrifty Fun. https://www.thriftyfun.com/tf/Food_Tips_and_Info/Canning/Canning-Kiwifruit.html

Bir, S. (2022, May 11). *New to canning? Here's what you need to know.* Simply Recipes. https://www.simplyrecipes.com/water-bath-canning-for-beginners-5271744

Bynum, L. (2019, June 6). *The basics of water bath canning.* The Cooking Bride. https://cookingbride.com/kitchen-basics/water-bath-canning/

Canning grapefruit. (n.d.). Ball Mason Jars. https://www.ballmasonjars.com/blog?cid=canning-grapefruit-ballr-canning-recipes

Carter, B. (n.d.). *The preppers pantry: Essentials of emergency food storage.* US Preppers. https://uspreppers.com/the-preppers-pantry-essentials-of-emergency-food-storage/

Cery. (2018, April 23). *Decadent spiced plums {a canning recipe}*. Back to Our Roots. https://www.backtoourroots.net/spiced-plums

Conte, C. (2013, July 25). *When life gives you figs, make fig jam...orange fig jam*. Christina's Cucina. https://www.christinascucina.com/when-life-gives-you-figs-make-fig-jam/

Davis, A. (2018, May 7). *Water bath canning equipment*. Frugal Living NW. https://www.frugallivingnw.com/water-bath-canning-collecting-the-right-equipment/

EatingWell Editors. (2020, August 20). *10 Steps to Water-Bath Canning*. EatingWell. https://www.eatingwell.com/article/15855/10-steps-to-water-bath-canning/

Fikes, T. (2017, April 15). *59 Water bath canning recipes to try today*. Survival Sullivan. https://www.survivalsullivan.com/water-bath-canning-recipes/

Gordon, B. (2021, February). *3 Strategies for successful meal planning*. Eat Right. https://www.eatright.org/food/planning-and-prep/smart-shopping/3-strategies-for-successful-meal-planning

Grey, M. I. (2020, December 14). *Prepper pantry: 20 Essentials to stockpile*. Survival Sullivan. https://www.survivalsullivan.com/prepper-pantry-essentials/

Grow a Good Life. (2022, June 6). *Pickled garlic canning recipe*. https://growagoodlife.com/pickled-garlic/

Haas, S. (2019, January 30). *Meal preppin' in the pantry*. Plan to Eat. https://www.plantoeat.com/blog/2019/01/meal-preppin-pantry-2/

Happy Preppers. (n.d.). *Prepper pantry list*. https://www.happypreppers.com/preppers-pantry.html

Harbour, S. (2022, March 27). *15 Best prepper pantries and tips on stocking your own*. An off Grid Life. https://www.anoffgridlife.com/best-prepper-pantries/

Healthy Canning. (n.d.-a). *Water bath canning theory*. https://www.healthycanning.com/water-bath-canning-theory/

Healthy Canning. (n.d.-b). *Water bath canning: Step by step*. https://www.healthycanning.com/water-bath-canning-step-by-step

Healthy Canning. (2015b, August 18). *Sweet corn relish.* https://www.healthycanning.com/sweet-corn-relish

Healthy Canning. (2016a, January 2). *Marinated Mushrooms.* https://www.healthycanning.com/marinated-mushrooms

Healthy Canning. (2017a, September 1). *Tomato-vegetable juice blend.* https://www.healthycanning.com/tomato-vegetable-juice-blend

Hill, A. (2019, July 8). *How to meal plan: 23 Helpful tips.* Healthline. https://www.healthline.com/nutrition/meal-prep-tips

Hill, B. (2018, September 4). *Pickled carrots with dill and garlic.* Dish "N" the Kitchen. https://dishnthekitchen.com/pickled-carrots-with-dill-and-garlic/

Hobby Farms. (2021, August 12). *What items should you stock in your prepper pantry?* https://www.hobbyfarms.com/what-items-should-you-stock-in-your-prepper-pantry/

Homestead Dreamer. (2016, November 7). *5 Things you should never water bath can.* http://www.homesteaddreamer.com/2016/11/07/5-things-you-should-never-water-bath-can/

J&R Pierce Family Farm. (n.d.). *The ultimate list of what you can (And cannot!) can.* J&R Pierce Family Farm: Official Blog. https://www.jrpiercefamilyfarm.com/2019/08/15/the-ultimate-list-of-what-you-can-and-cannot-can/

Jennifer. (2016, March 5). *Wholegrain mustard - a water bath food preservation recipe.* Vintage Mountain Homestead. https://oneacrevintagehome.com/wholegrain-mustard-canning/

Johnston, C. (2018, July 23). *Canning salted cantaloupe jam.* Wholefully. https://wholefully.com/canning-salted-cantaloupe-jam/

Kazan, S. (2021, September 21). *A step-by-step guide to water bath canning for beginners.* Alphafoodie. https://www.alphafoodie.com/a-step-by-step-guide-to-water-bath-canning-for-beginners/

Lockcuff, M. (2020, March 11). *Beginner's guide to stocking a working prepper pantry.* Adventures of Mel. https://adventuresofmel.com/beginners-guide-to-stocking-a-working-prepper-pantry/

Magyar, C. (2020, July 14). *15 Potentially dangerous canning mistakes & how to avoid them.* Rural Sprout. https://www.ruralsprout.com/canning-mistakes/

Maria. (2019, July 10). *Canning raw pack whole tomatoes - a step by step guide.* She Loves Biscotti. https://www.shelovesbiscotti.com/canning-raw-pack-whole-tomatoes/

McClellan, M. (2018, October 29). *Pear vanilla caramel sauce.* Food in Jars. https://foodinjars.com/recipe/pear-vanilla-caramel-sauce/

Meredith, L. (2020, September 17). *Boiling water bath and pressure canning - when to use which.* The Spruce Eats. https://www.thespruceeats.com/boiling-water-bath-versus-pressure-canning-1327438

Molina, M. (n.d.). *Sauerkraut for canning.* Allrecipes. https://www.allrecipes.com/recipe/21154/sauerkraut-for-canning/

Mountain Feed & Farm Supply. (n.d.-a). *How to make old fashioned ketchup: Preservative and additive free.* https://www.mountainfeed.com/blogs/learn/40577089-how-to-make-old-fashioned-ketchup-preservative-and-additive-free

Mountain Feed & Farm Supply. (n.d.-b). *Our must-have list of canning equipment & supplies.* Https://www.mountainfeed.com/blogs/learn/15522713-our-must-have-list-of-canning-equipment-supplies

National Center for Home Food Preservation. (n.d.-a). *Barbecue sauce.* https://nchfp.uga.edu/how/can_03/bbqsauce.html

National Center for Home Food Preservation. (2003, August). *How do I? Can salsa.* https://nchfp.uga.edu/how/can_salsa/peach_apple_salsa.html

Norman, C. L. (2002). *SP325-A food preservation methods of canning.* https://trace.tennessee.edu/cgi/viewcontent.cgi?article=1004&context=utk_agexfood

Norris, M. (2022, July 10). *How to can apricots - easy canned apricots recipe.* Melissa K. Norris. https://melissaknorris.com/howtocanapricotscanned-apricots-recipe/

Paa, A. (2021, September 9). *Hot pepper jelly recipe (For canning)*. Heartbeet Kitchen. https://heartbeetkitchen.com/hot-pepper-jelly-recipe/

Penn State Extension. (2019, May 13). *Approved canning methods: Types of canners*. https://extension.psu.edu/approved-canning-methods-types-of-canners

Penn State Extension. (2020, August 31). *Foods that are not safe to can*. https://extension.psu.edu/foods-that-are-not-safe-to-can

Peterson, A. (2022, June 2). *Garlicky pickled mixed veggies*. Better Homes & Gardens. https://www.bhg.com/recipe/garlicky-pickled-mixed-veggies/

Peterson, S. (2021a, March 30). *Canning cherries: Great for quick cobblers, pies, or over ice cream!* Simply Canning. https://www.simplycanning.com/canning-cherries/

Peterson, S. (2022, July 14). *Water bath canning with printable checklist. How to use your canner*. SimplyCanning. https://www.simplycanning.com/water-bath-canning/

Phelan, K. (2019, August 29). *4 Canning dangers to be aware of*. Homestead Survival Site. https://homesteadsurvivalsite.com/canning-dangers/

Pierce, R. (2019a, September 21). *How to can pickled onions – the easiest method*. The Homesteading Hippy. https://thehomesteadinghippy.com/canned-pickled-onions/

Pierce, R. (2019b, November 15). *How to can pickled eggplant step by step*. The Homesteading Hippy. https://thehomesteadinghippy.com/canning-pickled-eggplant/

Polanco, J. (2020, March 23). *What is a prepper pantry and why should you consider starting one?* Julie Naturally. https://www.julienaturally.com/what-is-prepper-pantry/

Pressure Canners. (2018, May 12). *The guide to water bath canning*. https://pressurecanners.com/water-bath-canning/

Rachel. (2015, August 19). *Small batch crunchy canned dill pickles*. Simple Seasonal. https://simpleseasonal.com/recipes/specific-audiences/canning/small-batch-crunchy-canned-dill-pickles

Radaich, M. (n.d.). *Mint jelly*. Food Preserving. http://www.foodpreserving.org/2012/09/mint-jelly.html

Road to Reliance. (2022, March 25). *How to start a prepper pantry - a complete guide.* https://roadtoreliance.com/how-to-start-a-prepper-pantry/

Rose, S. (2020, April 23). *What is a prepper pantry and why should you consider starting one?* Rurally Prepping. https://rurallyprepping.com/prepper-pantry/

Sakawsky, A. (2019, July 6). *Water bath canning for beginners.* The House & Homestead. https://thehouseandhomestead.com/water-bath-canning-beginners/

Sarah. (2019, July 2). *Canning peaches {How to can peaches}.* Sustainable Cooks. https://www.sustainablecooks.com/canning-peaches/

SB Canning. (n.d.-a). *Canning mixed fruit - better in a jar!* https://www.sbcanning.com/2013/03/canning-mixed-fruit-better-in-jar.html

SB Canning. (2016, December 9). *Pecan pie filling {canning recipe}.* https://www.cookingwithmaryandfriends.com/2016/12/pecan-pie-filling-canning-recipe.html

SBCanning. (n.d.). *Four recipe Monday - (1st) green tomato Chutney.* https://www.sbcanning.com/2011/08/four-recipe-monday-1st-green-tomato.html

SDSU Extension. (2022, June 30). *Water bathing vs. pressure canning.* https://extension.sdstate.edu/water-bathing-vs-pressure-canning

Shaw, K. (2022a, April 24). *Triple berry jam for canning.* Heart's Content Farmhouse. https://heartscontentfarmhouse.com/triple-berry-jam/

Shaw, K. (2022b, July 15). *Candied jalapeños for canning {recipe + video}.* Heart's Content Farmhouse. https://heartscontentfarmhouse.com/cowboy-candy-for-canning/

Taste of Home Test Kitchen. (n.d.-b). *Watermelon jelly.* Taste of Home. https://www.tasteofhome.com/recipes/watermelon-jelly/

The Grateful Girl Cooks! (2015, January 30). *Chocolate raspberry sundae sauce.* https://www.thegratefulgirlcooks.com/chocolate-raspberry-sundae-sauce/

Thomas, C. (2020a, January 29). *Step by step tutorial for canning meat (Raw rack nethod).* Homesteading Family. https://homesteadingfamily.com/step-by-step-tutorial-for-canning-meat-raw-pack-method/

Thomas, C. (2020b, September 4). *Canning mistakes to avoid (For water bath & pressure canning)*. Homesteading Family. https://homesteadingfamily.com/canning-mistakes-to-avoid/

Toney, S. (n.d.). *Mint jelly*. The Free Range Life. http://www.foodpreserving.org/2012/09/mint-jelly.html

Toney, S. (2018a, October 1). *Canning applesauce - super easy homemade applesauce!* The Free Range Life. https://thefreerangelife.com/homemade-applesauce/

Toney, S. (2018b, October 14). *21 Foods you can preserve in a water bath canner (So easy!)*. The Free Range Life. https://thefreerangelife.com/foods-water-bath-canner/

Treadaway, A., & Crayton, E. F. (2019, May 21). *Wise methods of canning vegetables*. Alabama Cooperative Extension System. https://www.aces.edu/blog/topics/food-safety/wise-methods-of-canning-vegetables/Troutman, E. (2020, April 9). *The dangers of water bath canning vegetables*. Burke County Center. https://burke.ces.ncsu.edu/2020/04/the-dangers-of-water-bath-canning-vegetables/

University of Georgia. (2019, August). *Preserving food: Jams and jellies*. https://nchfp.uga.edu/publications/uga/uga_jams_jellies.pdf

Victoria. (2022, May 21). *Beginner's guide to water bath canning*. A Modern Homestead. https://www.amodernhomestead.com/homestead-skills-water-bath-canning/

Vinskofski, S. (2020, July 6). *Homemade hot pepper sauce with instructions for canning*. Learning and Yearning. https://learningandyearning.com/hot-pepper-sauce/

Vuković, D. (2019, May 21). *Water bath canning instructions & safety tips*. Primal Survivor. https://www.primalsurvivor.net/water-bath-canning/

Wahome, C. (2021, August 16). *How to can meat and poultry at home*. WebMD. https://www.webmd.com/food-recipes/features/how-to-can-meat-and-poultry-at-home

Welch, S. (2018, September 20). *Apple pie filling*. Dinner at the Zoo. https://www.dinneratthezoo.com/apple-pie-filling/

Wholesome Farmhouse Recipes. (2021, January 14). *Canning old-fashioned pickled beets.* https://wholesomefarmhouserecipes.com/canning-old-fashioned-pickled-beets/

Winger, J. (2014, September 19). *How to can pears without sugar.* The Prairie Homestead. **https://www.theprairiehomestead.com/2014/09/how-to-can-pears-without-sugar.html**

Image References

APA   Aceron,   E.   (2020).   *[Meat]*.   Unsplash.   [Image].
https://unsplash.com/photos/YlAmh_X_SsE

Babali,   S.   (2021).   *Cherries   on   Red   Background*.   Unsplash.   [Image].
https://unsplash.com/photos/HUih6WfsZzM

Claire,   R.   (2020).   *Top   View   of   Apple   Pie*.   Pexels.   [Image].
https://www.pexels.com/photo/top-view-of-apple-pie-5863603/

Claire,   R.   (2021).   *Person   Carrying   a   Hot   Pot*.   Pexels.   [Image].
https://www.pexels.com/photo/person-carrying-a-hot-pot-6752363/

Elevate.   (2018).   *[Wholegrain   Mustard]*.   Unsplash.   [Image].
https://unsplash.com/photos/YtzVxO9NFjc

Escu, A. (2021). *[Pot]*. Unsplash. [Image]. https://unsplash.com/photos/ZaVV6TF7R10

Grachev,   R.   (2020).   *[Vegetables]*.   Unsplash.   [Image].
https://unsplash.com/photos/eygJ8wxgfng

Henderson,   G.   (2018).   *Mellow   Yellow*.   Unsplash.   [Image].
https://unsplash.com/photos/5HqtJT2l9Gw

Hutter,   R.   (2020).   *Time   Timer   Watch*.   Unsplash.   [Image].
https://unsplash.com/photos/xLs4XSQmxtE

Klein,   D.   (2016).   *Fresh   Tomato   Sauce*.   Unsplash.   [Image].
https://unsplash.com/photos/FzB_512zvP0

Labenord. (2015). *Jams Marmalades Farmers Market Homemade Preserves*. Pixabay. [Image].
https://pixabay.com/photos/jams-marmalades-farmers-market-997593/

Leung,   J.   (2018).   *[No   Labels]*.   Unsplash.   [Image].
https://unsplash.com/photos/19pdhEmwkBU

Meintjes,   S.   (2020).   *Mint,   Herb,   Herbs*.   Unsplash.   [Image].
https://unsplash.com/photos/dJ4JgX5I5y8

Pixabay. (2017). *Clear Glass Mason Jars*. Pexels. [Image]. https://www.pexels.com/photo/clear-glass-mason-jars-48817/

Riggs, S. (2022). *[Pickled Carrots]*. Unsplash. [Image]. https://unsplash.com/photos/RhWNvFxZ0Hg

Shimazaki, S. (2020). *Woman Suffering from a Stomach Pain Lying Down on Couch*. Pexels. [Image]. https://www.pexels.com/photo/woman-suffering-from-a-stomach-pain-lying-down-on-couch-5938365/

Shrewsberry, R. (2021). *Old-Fashioned Root Cellar Showing Preserved Food in Glass Jars*. Unsplash. [Image]. https://unsplash.com/photos/bhni1zsPiio

Yahsi, A. (2020). *[Pickling]*. Unsplash. [Image]. https://unsplash.com/photos/4rPoNLW_3rs

Z Grills Australia. (2020). *Brushing BBQ Sauce on Racks of Ribs in a Z Grill Pellet Smoker*. Unsplash. [Image]. https://unsplash.com/photos/pZyDC7BVN7s

Zolotova, J. (2021). *[Fruits]*. Unsplash. [Image]. https://unsplash.com/photos/M_xIaxQE3Ms